SRA

Reading Mastery

Signature Edition

Textbook

Siegfried Engelmann
Owen Engelmann
Karen Lou Seitz Davis

Columbus, OH

SRAonline.com

 **SRA**

Printed in the United States of America.

Send all inquiries to this address:
SRA/McGraw-Hill
4400 Easton Commons
Columbus, OH 43219

ISBN: 978-0-07-612460-2
MHID: 0-07-612460-6

8 9 10 QDB 13 12 11

Table of Contents for Stories

1. race
2. push
3. friend
4. motor

1. smoke
2. smoky
3. swim
4. swimmer
5. dump
6. dumpy

1. rag
2. brag
3. bragged
4. bragging

1. honk
2. strong
3. contest
4. racket

1. tug
2. bay
3. boat
4. sleek
5. noon

The Bragging Rats

A pack of rats lived on a farm. Their home was not far from the pond.

There were two rats in the pack who made the other rats angry. These two rats did a lot of bragging and a lot of yelling at each other. They did not agree on which rat was the best at throwing, or which rat was the fastest at eating. These rats told a lot of lies. The other rats called them the bragging rats.

One time, the bragging rats did not agree on which rat was the fastest swimmer. One rat said, "I can swim so fast that I pass up seals and otters."

The other rat said, "I can swim so fast I don't get wet."

As the two rats were standing next to the pond and bragging, it started to rain. The rain turned the dirt near the pond into mud. Before the bragging rats knew what was happening, they slipped into the pond. They were not able to get out. One rat said, “Help. This pond is too deep for me.”

The other rats said, “We will help you get out, but you must stop saying how well you swim.” The bragging rats agreed. After that, they never bragged about how well they swam. But they bragged about lots of other things.

The end.

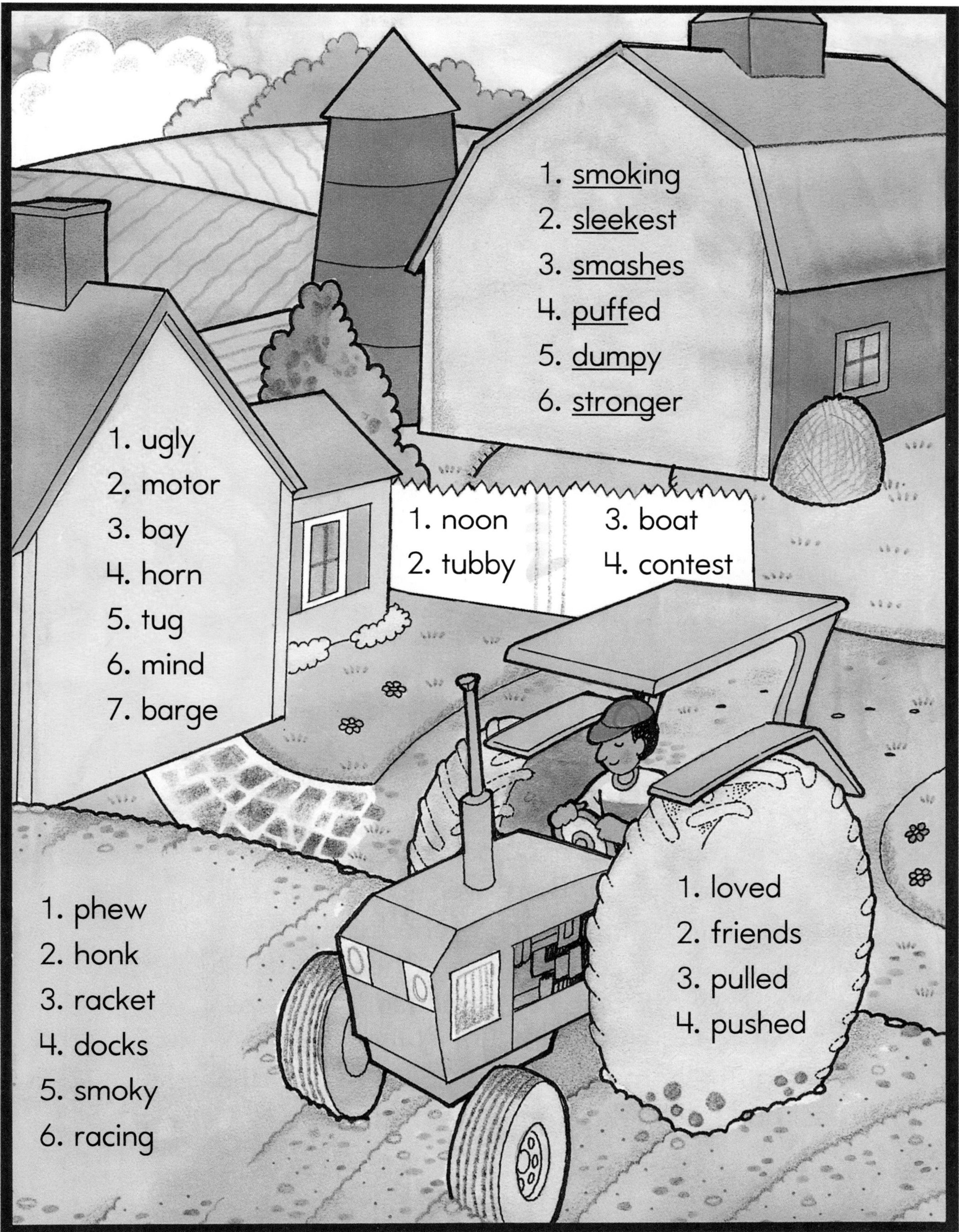
1. smoking
2. sleekest
3. smashes
4. puffed
5. dumpy
6. stronger
1. ugly
2. motor
3. bay
4. horn
5. tug
6. mind
7. barge
1. noon
2. tubby
3. boat
4. contest
1. phew
2. honk
3. racket
4. docks
5. smoky
6. racing
1. loved
2. friends
3. pulled
4. pushed

Tubby the Tug
Part One

Bay Town got its name because it was on a big bay. Many, many ships and boats came in and out of that bay every day. There were boats with sails and boats with motors. Some of the fastest motorboats stayed at Dock Three. Those boats loved to show off. Each boat bragged that it was the fastest and the sleekest. But all the boats knew that the boat named Red Cat was really the fastest and the sleekest.

All the other boats wanted to be friends with Red Cat. They liked to be seen near Red Cat. But those boats couldn't keep up with Red Cat when that boat was going at his fastest speed. When Red Cat was going as fast as he could go, no other boat in the bay could keep up with him. Red Cat would dart around the barges and the slower ships.

Sometimes Red Cat would get very close to them, and they would blow their horns. But Red Cat didn't mind if the other boats got mad. What could they do about it?

One of the boats at Dock Three was as slow as Red Cat was fast. That boat was as dumpy as Red Cat was sleek. That boat was a smoky old tug named Tubby. All the other boats said "phew" when Tubby puffed in and out of the bay to do her work.

Most of the other boats were fun boats, but Tubby was a work boat. Tubby was ten times slower than Red Cat, but she was ten times stronger than Red Cat. Tubby's job was to pull and push the biggest ships in the bay.

Tubby was almost as strong as those large ships. And Tubby needed to be strong to keep the large ships from running into things. Tubby had to steer them away from the places where the bay was not deep. Tubby had to keep them from ramming into the docks. If a large ship runs into the docks, it keeps right on going and smashes everything before it finally stops.

This is not the end.

TUBBY
WAVE RUNNER
Phew.
RED CAT

Peggy wanted to paint her porch pink. So she got three pails of pink paint and some brushes. Peggy asked two of her pals to come and help her paint.

Each girl had a brush and a can of pink paint. Peggy started with the front of the house, and her two pals painted the floor.

When they were done, Peggy was standing in the only part of the porch that wasn't pink. "Help, help," Peggy said. "I'm stuck on the porch."

Peggy's pals laughed. "You will have to stay there until the porch is dry."

But Peggy did not want to stay. She painted the part that wasn't pink. Then she walked across the wet paint. Now the porch is pink, and Peggy's feet are pink.

1. What did Peggy want to paint?
2. Peggy wanted to paint it ▬.
3. Peggy said, "I'm ▬ on the porch."
4. How did Peggy get across the wet paint?
5. Now what things are pink?

3

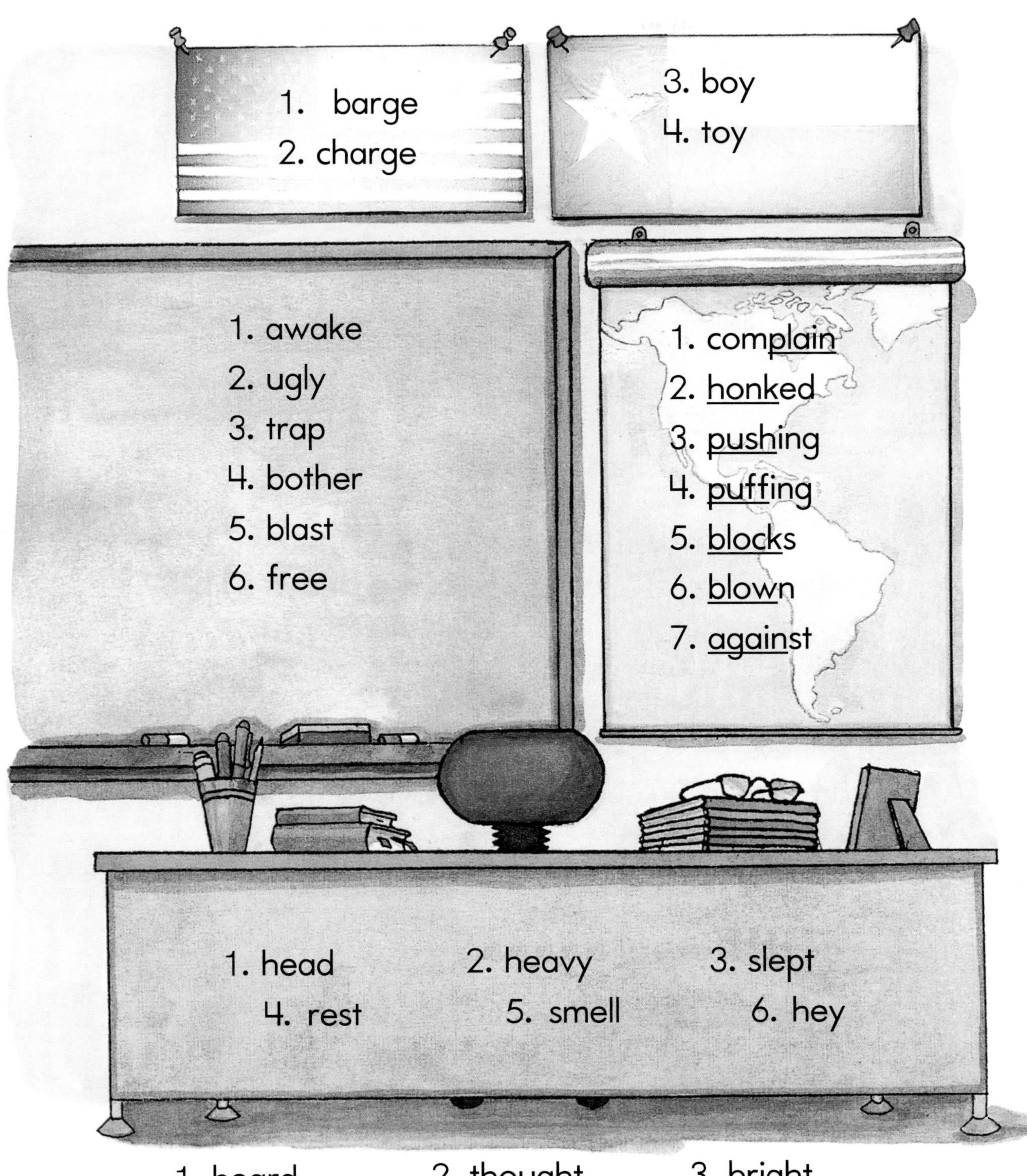

1. heard 2. thought 3. bright

Tubby the Tug
Part Two

It was six o'clock in the morning, and Tubby was starting her motor and puffing out smoke. The other boats at the dock woke up and started complaining. "We're trying to rest," they said. "What are you making all that racket for—and all that smoke? Phew."

"I can't help it," Tubby said. "I have to go to work."

"Well, go," Red Cat said. "And don't come back. I can't even nap when you're around. You smell bad."

So Tubby honked her horn three times and went off to push and pull the big ships in and out of the bay. The other boats got mad when Tubby honked her horn, but Tubby kept telling them, "I have to honk my horn three times when I start work, and three times when I stop."

Around noon, the other boats at Dock Three came out to play. They darted around the bay and made waves. They laughed as they chased each other.

Tubby watched them, but only once in a while. The rest of the time, she had to watch what she was doing and where she was pushing ships and barges.

Once in a while, two or three of the fast boats would speed past Tubby and say something like, “Tubby, do you want to race?”

That would make Tubby feel bad. Tubby knew that a race with those boats would not be much of a contest. Tubby would go only a hundred feet in the time the other boats would go a mile.

So Tubby worked, and the others played. And at the end of the day, when Tubby had put the last ship in place, she would honk her horn three times and go back to Dock Three. Tubby tried to keep her motor quiet so she wouldn’t make too much smoke, but the other boats complained. “This is a no smoking dock,” one of them yelled. “Get that smoking tug out of here.”

One of the very sleek boats said to the boat next to it, “There goes one ugly boat. Phew.”

Tubby went to the end of the dock and tried to rest. It wouldn’t be long before Tubby had to go to work again.

More to come.

No smoking here.
TUBBY

Dave and Bob were going to a party that their friend Jan was having. Bob and Dave were picking things to give Jan. Dave said to Bob, "Jan will like what I give her more than she will like what you give her."

Bob said, "I do not care if Jan likes what you give her better. I just hope she likes all of her presents."

The day of the party, Jan and Dave and five of their friends were at the party. They were waiting for Bob to come before they cut the cake. Bob was late.

At last Bob came, and they had cake. After everyone was done eating the cake, Jan opened the things her friends brought her. Did she like what Dave brought her more? No. Dave and Bob gave her the same thing.

1. Whose party were Bob and Dave going to?
2. Who wanted Jan to like all of her presents?
3. What did they wait to do until Bob got there?
4. Why didn't Jan like Dave's present more than Bob's present?

1. tow 2. free 3. burn
4. thought 5. heard
1. blasts
2. blocks
3. blown
4. trapped
1. crashed
2. lashed
3. smashed
4. bashed
1. moved
2. between
3. awake
4. against
5. bumping
6. bothering
7. toys
1. heavy
2. slept
3. heading
4. very

Tubby the Tug
Part Three

That night, when Tubby and the other boats at Dock Three were sleeping, a very bad storm raced into the bay. The winds lashed out and rolled the water into large waves. Soon those waves were crashing against the docks. They were also crashing against the ships and barges. One barge that was longer than three blocks was blown out of place.

The wind and waves were pushing that barge right at Dock Three. Most of the speed boats were awake now, but the crashing waves had them trapped next to the dock. One of them saw the barge coming closer and closer to the dock. "Help, help," that boat called out. "Who can help me get free?"

The other boats were tugging at their ropes and shouting at each other. "Stop bumping into me," Red Cat shouted to the boat next to him.

"I can't help it," that boat said. "The waves are pushing me into you."

While all this was going on, Tubby was sleeping. All the wind and the waves were not bothering that old tug boat. She rocked a little, but she was ten times as heavy as the other boats and didn't mind wind and waves. So she slept.

The barge was very close to the dock now. It was so big that it made the dock look very small and made those boats look like little toys.

Then the barge made three loud horn blasts. Honk, honk, honk. It was trying to let everybody know that it was heading for the dock.

Those blasts woke Tubby. When Tubby heard them, she thought it was time to go to work. So Tubby quickly started her motor and let out three horn blasts. Red Cat and the others heard Tubby's blasts and saw the smoke. "Help us, Tubby. We're going to be smashed. Help us."

"Wow," Tubby said when she saw how close the barge was. "I don't know if I can stop that barge in time."

"Oh, please try. Please," the other boats cried.

More next time.

Last summer, Ted had a job picking apples. Ted picked apples all day long. He picked red apples, and he picked green apples. Ted tried not to pick apples that had holes in them or apples that had brown spots.

Every day after work, Ted got to take home all the apples he wanted. He ate some of the apples. With other apples, he made pies. He put the rest of them in jars and cans. Ted loved picking apples and eating them.

1. What was Ted's job?
2. Did Ted like his job?
3. Were all of the apples good apples?
4. What did Ted get to take home with him?

aw gh ge ce ch qu ou
1. boil
2. join
3. point
4. voice
MILK
1. course
2. act
3. sneak
4. mouse
5. gray
6. tease
1. music
2. merry
3. together
4. awful
5. between
6. tow
7. burn
1. ice
2. nice
3. mice
4. pounce
5. fence
1. mountain
2. valley
3. smash
4. moved
5. moving
6. bright

Tubby the Tug
Part Four

A large barge was coming right at Dock Three. If something didn't stop that barge very soon, the barge would smash Red Cat and the other boats. "Help," Red Cat cried. "Please save us."

Tubby was trying to do that. The tug puffed out smoke and went as fast as she could. Honk, honk, honk. But the barge kept moving closer and closer to Dock Three.

Tubby went between the barge and the dock. Then Tubby pushed against the side of the barge as hard as she could. But the barge didn't stop. It was now very close to the motorboats.

Tubby kept pushing and puffing and puffing and pushing. And the barge started moving slower and slower. Then it stopped. Then it moved slowly back. Tubby was pushing that barge against the waves and the wind. The other boats saw what Tubby was doing.

"Tubby saved us," Red Cat shouted.

The boats cheered and shouted, but Tubby still had a lot of work to do. After a long time, Tubby pushed that barge way out in the bay where it should be.

Tubby's motor worked so hard that parts of it started to burn up. When the barge was finally in place, Tubby stopped out there in the bay. Honk, honk, honk. The other boats knew that Tubby's motor had blown up.

"I'll save Tubby," Red Cat said as he got free from the dock. Red Cat raced out into the bay, grabbed Tubby's tow rope, and pulled the little tug back to the dock. Red Cat never worked so hard before, but he was glad to do it.

Today, Tubby's motor is fixed. And Tubby has a coat of bright red paint, just like Red Cat. And Tubby has a place right next to Red Cat at Dock Three. Tubby still honks and puffs smoke and goes to work every morning. But the other boats don't complain. And no boats make fun of Tubby as they speed by. They wave and say the things that pals say when they see each other. "How are you doing?" They are proud to have Tubby as their friend.

The end.

There was a barge that didn't like tug boats. The barge said, "Those tugs are always bumping into my side and trying to push me around."

One day, the barge was going into a bay when a tug boat came near. The barge said, "I don't need your help. I can find a good place in the bay by myself."

Just then a big wind pushed the barge all the way to the shore. "Help, help," the barge called. "Who can move me away from the shore?"

The tug said, "I could do it. But you'll have to be nice to me." The barge agreed. So the tug pulled the barge away from the shore. Now the tug and the barge are good friends.

1. Who did not like tugs?
2. Who said, "I don't need your help"?
3. A wind came up when the barge was heading into a ______.
4. That wind pushed the barge all the way to the ______.
5. Where did the tug pull the barge?

1. sounded
2. following
3. mountains
4. valleys
5. anywhere
6. painting

1. phone
2. of course
3. moving
4. lovely
5. robot

1. point
2. voice
3. boil

1. spoke
2. wash
3. awful
4. together
5. merry
6. music

1. sneak
2. speak
3. ray
4. gray
5. nice
6. mice

1. slices
2. people
3. perfect
4. toaster

Rolla Slows Down

Rolla was very happy. She was horse number 1 on a merry-go-round. She went up and down with the music. The children were happy, and their mothers were happy.

Things went on like this for weeks. But then one day, something happened. Rolla said to herself, "I am number 1, but I am right behind number 8." Rolla thought that she should be far away from number 8. Then it would look as if she was the leader and the other horses were following her.

Rolla said, "I will get far from horse 8." To do that, Rolla slowed down. She went slower, and slower, and slower. But of course her plan didn't work. When she went slower, all the other horses went slower. The music slowed down and sounded awful. The mothers were unhappy. One of them said, "This merry-go-round is so slow, you can't tell if it's going or if it has stopped."

The other horses were not happy with Rolla. Horse 2 kept shouting at Rolla, "Come on, Rolla. Let's get this merry-go-round moving." But Rolla tried as hard as she could to slow down.

At the end of the day, horse 8 was still there, right in front of her.

That evening, horse number 3 asked, "What are you trying to do?"

When Rolla told them, some of the horses started to laugh. Then horse number 5 said, "Rolla, would you be happy if you could not see horse 8?"

"Yes," Rolla said. "If I could not see that horse, I would not feel like I was following it. I would feel like the leader."

So the other horses got together and did a lot of talking. When they were done, they smiled and told Rolla they would fix things up.

The next day when Rolla woke up, she looked in front of her and saw mountains and valleys. They were lovely. She couldn't see another horse anywhere in front of her. After a while, she found out that the other horses had made a painting and put it between her and horse 8. But Rolla didn't care. She felt wonderful leading the other horses into the mountains.

So everything is fine now. The horses are happy. The music sounds good. And the mothers and children like the merry-go-round even more than before.

The end.

A boy named Ted was always thinking. He would think in the morning. He would think when he ate lunch. He would think in school and at home. One day, his sister said to him, "Why do you spend so much time thinking?"

Ted said, "I don't know. Let me think about that."

So Ted thought about why he thought. This went on for five days.

Then he told his sister, "I don't know why I think so much. But I think I'm tired of thinking. Let's do something else."

So they went bike riding.

1. Who always thought?
2. He thought at home and in ______.
3. Who asked him why he thought so much?
4. Did Ted know why he thought so much?
5. What did Ted and his sister do after Ted got tired of thinking?

oi ea ou ge gh ce
1. mice
2. slice
3. voice
4. choice
1. washing
2. corner
3. recall
4. dishes
5. toaster
1. Molly
2. Bleep
3. perfect
4. robot
5. hello
6. hung
1. elm
2. mess
3. people
4. phone
5. tigers
6. spoke
7. yum

Molly and Bleep Part One

Molly was a very smart woman. She made a lot of things that were very smart. She made toasters and folding chairs and even racing boats. But none of the things she made were perfect. Her toaster toasted six slices at the same time, but three of them were too dark. Her folding chairs folded when someone was sitting in them. One of Molly's pals was stuck in a folding chair for a long time before Molly found her.

Molly's racing boats were very fast and very strong. When they were going very fast, they were wonderful. But when they slowed down, they would get so low in the water that a little wave could sink them.

The best thing that Molly made was a robot named Bleep. She worked on Bleep every day in her shop. It took her six years to make that robot. When Molly was done, Bleep was almost perfect.

Bleep could get the mail, go to the store, and ride a bike. He could also do many things you told him to do. He could even speak. His voice sounded just like Molly's. But when Bleep spoke, he did two things that Molly did not do. Most of the time, Bleep started out by saying, "Bleep." And when someone told Bleep to do something, he would say, "Okay, baby."

Bleep could also talk on the phone and tell Molly what people said. If the phone rang while Molly was working on her folding chair or her racing boat, Bleep would talk on the phone. Later he would tell Molly what the person said. But Bleep would sometimes tell big lies. One time, Bleep talked on the phone and then said to Molly, "Bleep. Your mother just called. She found four tigers in the yard."

More to come.

Two ants named Tam and Sid lived far away from each other. They were best friends. But it took a lot of work to see each other, because they lived so far apart. One day, Tam would have to walk all the way to Sid's house and back. The next day, Sid would have to walk all the way to Tam's house and back. Those are very long walks for ants.

One day, Sid came up with a plan. Sid said, "We could both walk toward each other's house and meet somewhere in between. That way, we wouldn't have to walk as far."

So the ants tried that. But it didn't work. Sid didn't see Tam, and Tam didn't see Sid. Sid ended up at Tam's house, and Tam ended up at Sid's house.

1. Why did it take a lot of work for Tam and Sid to be best friends?

2. Where did Sid plan to meet Tam?

3. Did the plan work?

4. Where did Tam end up?

5. Where did Sid end up?

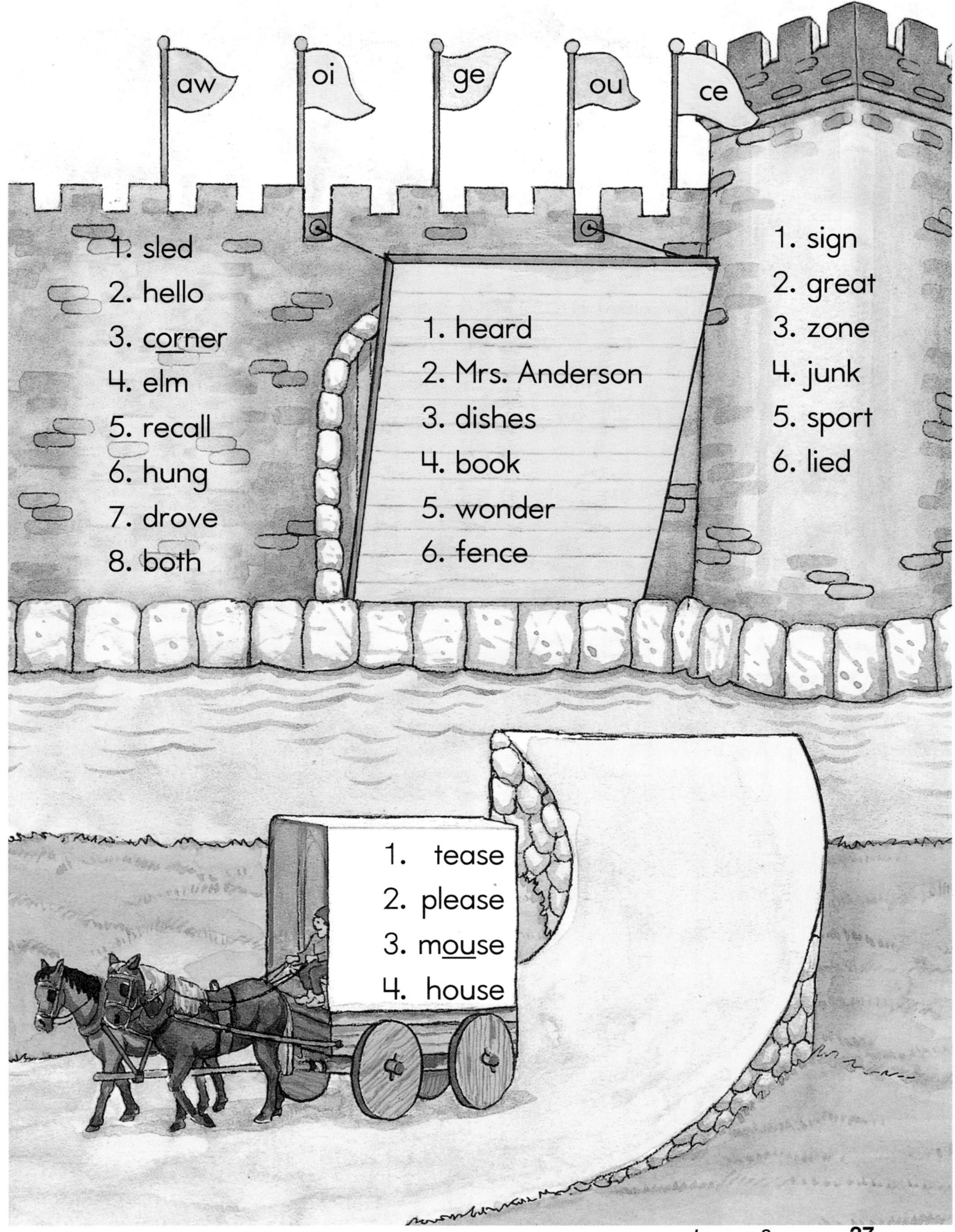
aw
oi
ge
ou
ce
1. sled
2. hello
3. corner
4. elm
5. recall
6. hung
7. drove
8. both
1. heard
2. Mrs. Anderson
3. dishes
4. book
5. wonder
6. fence
1. sign
2. great
3. zone
4. junk
5. sport
6. lied
1. tease
2. please
3. mouse
4. house

Molly and Bleep
Part Two

Bleep was a robot that was almost perfect. But he did one thing that was not perfect. Sometimes he told big lies. And sometimes those lies made a big mess. The biggest mess that Bleep made happened when Mrs. Anderson called. She was a friend of Molly's. She had never met Bleep or heard his voice. Molly was in her shop working on a racing sled. Bleep was washing the dishes. When the phone rang, Bleep picked it up and said, "Bleep. Hello."

Mrs. Anderson did not know that she was talking to Bleep. She thought she was talking to Molly. So she said, "You know that we are to meet for lunch today."

Bleep said, "Bleep. Yes."

Mrs. Anderson said, "Well, it is your turn to pick a place where we will eat. Where do you want to go?"

Bleep said, "Bleep. I like the place on the corner of First and Elm."

Mrs. Anderson said, "First and Elm? I don't recall anything on that corner."

Bleep said, "Bleep. It is a fine place. You will like it a lot."

Mrs. Anderson said, "Well then, I will see you on the corner of First and Elm around noon." Then she said, "Could you also bring that book you wanted me to read?"

Bleep said, "Okay, baby."

Bleep hung up the phone and went back to washing the dishes. Pretty soon, Molly came in from her shop. She asked, "Did anyone call for me?"

Bleep said, "Bleep. Yes. Mrs. Anderson called about lunch today."

"Good," Molly said. "Where does she want to eat?"

Bleep said, "Bleep. The corner of First and Elm."

Molly said, "First and Elm? I don't recall a place to eat on that corner."

Bleep said, "Bleep. Mrs. Anderson said that it is a wonderful place to eat. Yum, yum."

Molly said, "That sounds good. Did she say anything else?"

Bleep said, "Bleep. Mrs. Anderson says that you should bring one of your folding chairs."

Molly shook her head. "I wonder why she wants a chair."

More next time.

Sandy was not very good at math. When she wanted to make a six, she would make a nine. When she wanted to make a two, she would make a five. Sandy also had a hard time with math problems. If the problem said to add six and two, Sandy could not put down the right numbers. She would add nine and five.

Sandy was sad. She asked her teacher to help her with her math. So her teacher worked with Sandy. Now Sandy is very good in math. She no longer mixes up six and nine, or two and five. Before long, Sandy could work any math problem that her teacher gave. She could even add three numbers at a time.

1. What was Sandy poor at?
2. Which number did Sandy write for six?
3. Which number did Sandy write for two?
4. How did Sandy get better at math?
5. Who helped her?

9

ge ch sh th ce aw

1. moment
2. maker
3. lady
4. sign
5. zone
6. great
7. both
8. drove

1. family
2. whisper
3. matter
4. parked
5. pounce
6. choice
7. charge

1. rule
2. sorry
3. junk
4. sport
5. rods
6. act

Molly and Bleep Part Three

Bleep talked on the phone and told Mrs. Anderson one big lie. Then Bleep talked to Molly and told her two big lies.

Molly did not know why Mrs. Anderson wanted a folding chair, but Molly told Bleep to load the chair into her van. Molly loved her van. It was red, and it was big. So it had lots of room for the things that Molly needed when she made something like a racing sled or a cake maker.

Molly drove her red van to the corner of First and Elm. She didn't see a place to eat. She didn't see Mrs. Anderson's car. The only thing she saw was a big junk yard. So she parked her car by the fence in front of the junk yard. There was a sign on the fence. That sign said "Drop Off Zone." Molly didn't know what a drop off zone was.

She got out of her car and walked along Elm Street. She was looking for Mrs. Anderson or the place where they would eat. But all she saw was a great junk yard. Molly kept walking and looking for Mrs. Anderson's car. That car was very easy to see. It was a bright red car, just like Molly's van. But Mrs. Anderson's car was a small sport car, not a big van.

While Molly was looking for Mrs. Anderson, Mrs. Anderson drove up to the corner of First and Elm. She saw Molly's van in the drop off zone. So she parked next to the van. Then she got out and started to look for Molly. She said to herself, "It is hard to believe that there is a good place to eat on this street." But she walked down Elm Street. At last she saw Molly.

She called to Molly and said, "Where is there a place to eat around here?"

Molly said, "I don't know. Bleep said you wanted to come here."

"Not so," Mrs. Anderson said. "When we talked on the phone, you told me that you wanted to come here."

Molly said, "Oh dear. You didn't talk to me on the phone. You talked to Bleep. I think Bleep lied to both of us."

This is not the end.

Jane and her pals went to hear some singers who were really good. They all got into Jane's van and went down town. Lots of people were there to listen to the singers. When Jane and her pals sat down, it was just about time for the singing to start.

The singers came out and sang two songs. When they started the third song, one of them began to sneeze. Then the rest of them sneezed. They sneezed until the end of the song. Jane and her pals liked the sneezing song a lot. Then they started to sneeze, too. Before long, everybody was sneezing.

1. Who did Jane go with?
2. Who did they hear?
3. How many songs did they sing without sneezing?
4. Did Jane and her pals like the sneezing song?
5. What did everyone do after that song?

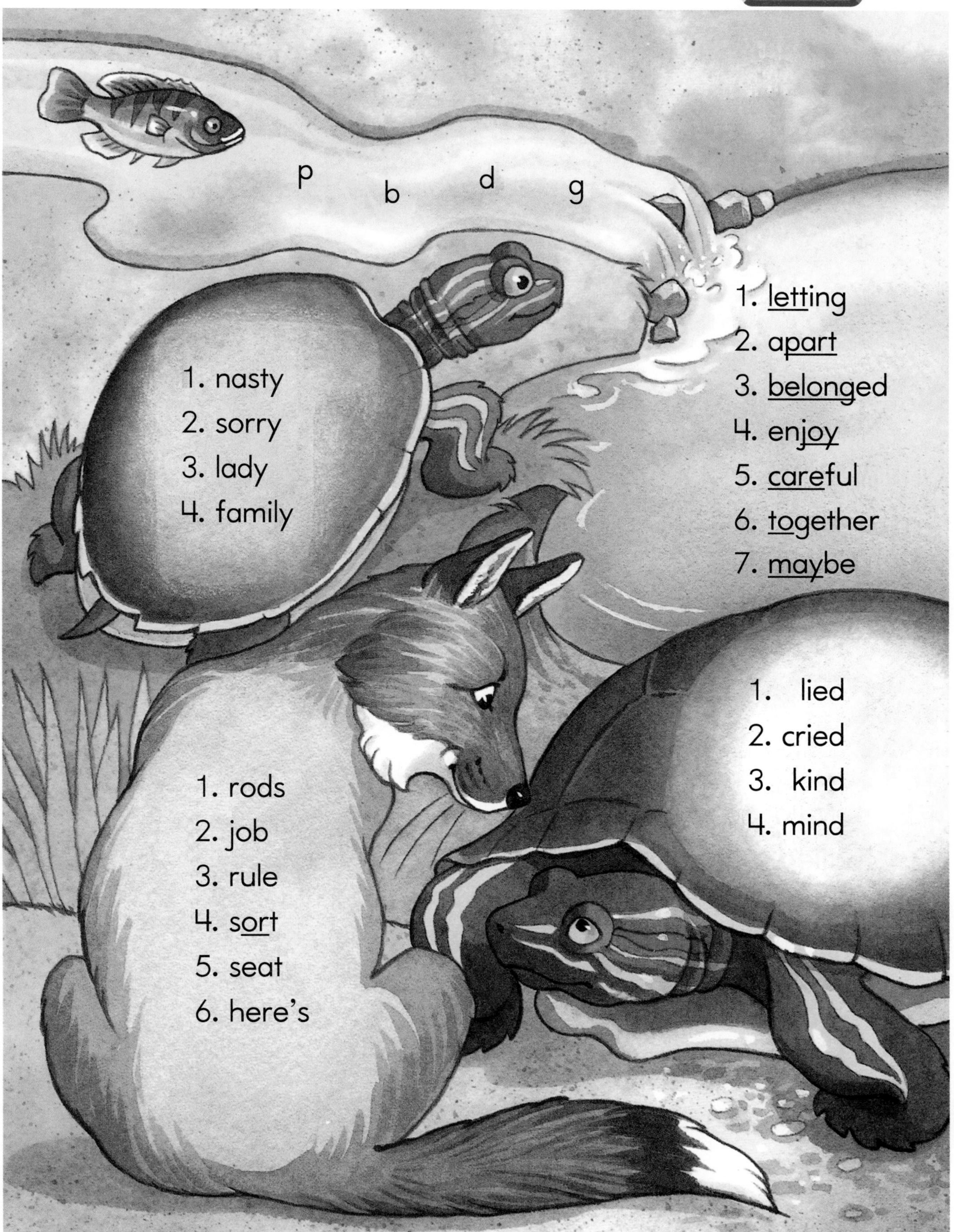
p b d g
1. letting
2. apart
3. belonged
4. enjoy
5. careful
6. together
7. maybe
1. nasty
2. sorry
3. lady
4. family
1. lied
2. cried
3. kind
4. mind
1. rods
2. job
3. rule
4. sort
5. seat
6. here's

Molly and Bleep
Part Four

Molly and Mrs. Anderson found out that Bleep had lied to both of them.

They laughed about it. Molly said, "I'll have to be careful about letting Bleep talk on the phone." Then Molly and Mrs. Anderson started to walk back to the corner of First and Elm.

When they got back to the drop off zone, Molly said, "Where is my van?"

Mrs. Anderson said, "Where is my car?"

Molly and Mrs. Anderson saw a worker, so they called to him and asked about the cars.

He said, "Here's the rule about the drop off zone. If cars are left in the drop off zone, we take them apart. Your cars were in the drop off zone. So your cars are no longer cars."

"No longer cars?" Mrs. Anderson shouted. "You can't take my car apart."

The worker said, "Sorry. We just followed the rule about cars in the drop off zone."

Then the worker led Molly and Mrs. Anderson inside the junk yard. He took them to a large pile of car parts. He said, "Well, this pile is what's left of your cars."

Mrs. Anderson said, "This is awful." She turned to the worker and said, "You took the cars apart, so now you can put them back together, just the way they were."

"Sorry, lady," the worker said. "We just take things apart. We don't know how to put them back together."

Mrs. Anderson started to cry.

Molly said, "I am pretty good at making things. If we can get some of the workers to help us, we can get these cars back together before it is time for dinner."

Four workers helped. Mrs. Anderson helped, too. Molly was in charge. She told the others where to put the rods and the doors and the other parts.

More to come.

Brett's family had a house on a lake. Last year, Brett's parents let his friend Mike stay with him for the week. The boys swam and went boating, hiking, and fishing. Soon it was time for Mike to go home. But Mike said, "I want to stay out here for the rest of the summer."

So Mike went to Brett's parents and said, "Can I stay out here if I do all the jobs around the house?"

They said yes. So Mike worked hard every morning to get his jobs done. Then he spent the rest of each day having fun with Brett. Everybody was happy.

1. Where was the house?

2. Who did Brett have come stay with him?

3. At first, how long was Mike going to stay?

4. How long did he stay?

5. Who had to do jobs around the house?

6. Was Mike happy?

1. sort
2. cheeks
3. afraid
4. job
5. tease
6. hall
1. food
2. tiny
3. family
4. putting
5. tickle
6. giggle
7. ugly
1. harder
2. maybe
3. moment
4. without
1. enjoy
2. belonged
3. tonight
4. together
5. party

Molly and Bleep Part Five

Molly, Mrs. Anderson, and four workers from the junk yard put the cars back together. By dinner time, there were two red cars inside the junk yard, but those two cars were not the same as the cars that drove up to the junk yard. There was no longer a van and a little sport car. There were two things that were part van and part sport car.

One of them looked like a van in front and a sport car in back. The other looked like a sport car in front and a van in back. That one had two seats and Molly's folding chair in it. Mrs. Anderson looked at the cars and started to cry again.

Molly said, "Well, I did the best I could, but all the parts were red. So I didn't always know which part belonged to which car."

The workers were laughing pretty hard. One of them said, "Those are two ugly cars."

Mrs. Anderson cried, "Yes, very ugly."

Molly said, "I don't know. I think those cars look sort of pretty."

The workers laughed harder than before.

Molly told Mrs. Anderson, "Well, pick one of these things, and I'll take the other."

So Mrs. Anderson drove home in one of the red things. At home she cried and cried. Molly drove home in the other red thing. Then she looked at it a long time and said to herself, "Those workers are right. This thing is ugly."

When Molly went inside, Bleep said, "Bleep. Did you enjoy lunch?"

Molly said, "No, I didn't." For a moment, she thought about taking Bleep back to the junk yard and leaving him in the drop off zone. But then she said, "From now on, you may not talk on the phone."

Bleep said, "Okay, baby."

The next day, three workers, Molly, and Bleep put the cars back together the right way. The workers were from a car shop. One of them was very good at putting cars together. He told Molly and the others where the parts went. When the job was done, Mrs. Anderson was very happy, and so was Molly.

The end.

GARAGE
EXPERT BODYWORK
OFFICE
They look great.
Oh, how wonderful.
Okay, baby.

A snail named Gail wanted to swim. She ran and jumped into a stream. Did she swim? No. She just sank to the bottom. She didn't have any arms or legs to swim with, so she had to creep along the bottom of the stream until she could get out of the water. That was no fun.

The next day, Gail tried to swim again. She went to another part of the stream and jumped in. Did she swim? No. She sank to the bottom of the stream. Gail just could not swim.

On the third day, Gail asked a turtle, "Could I sit on your back while you go swimming?"

The turtle said, "Yes." So Gail got on the turtle's back, and they went swimming. Gail said, "I knew I could swim if I just kept trying."

1. What did Gail want to do?

2. On the first day, what happened when Gail tried to swim?

3. What did she creep along to get out of the water?

4. Did she try to swim the next day?

5. Who helped Gail swim?

12

oi
ou
aw
dge
ce
ai
1. ew
2. new
3. chew
4. flew
1. Patty
2. Arnold
3. act
4. matter
5. room
6. boom
1. afraid
2. tonight
3. giggle
4. tickle
5. nasty
6. sister
1. whisper
2. loudly
3. snuck
4. gray
5. pounce
6. cheeks
7. teased

Patty and the Cats
Part One

There once was a very large mouse named Patty. She lived with her mom and dad and her six brothers and nine sisters.

All the other mice in her family were nice and quiet. Each one spoke in a tiny voice. When the house was dark at night, they snuck around without making a sound.

Patty did not act like the others in her family. She could not speak in a tiny voice. Even when she tried to speak in a whisper, her voice was loud.

When she went with the others at night, she spoke so loudly that she scared them. They were scared because a large gray cat named Arnold lived in the house. If Arnold found the mice while they were sneaking around looking for food, he would pounce on them. When Patty said something at night, her brothers and sisters would say, "Shshshsh." But no matter how hard she tried to talk quietly, her voice boomed out.

Patty's brothers gave her the name "Big Mouse the Big Mouth." She didn't like that name, but her voice was too loud. And if her brothers teased her too much, she could just say, "Please stop teasing me," and her voice would blow them over.

More next time.

Seth was a mouse who lived with his mother and father. His mother and father asked Seth to leave because he made messes and did not clean up. Seth walked around the forest looking for another place to live.

Seth found a mole who was living under the ground near a tree. Seth told the mole why he had to leave home. The mole told Seth, "I am good at cleaning up, but I don't know how to cook."

Seth said, "I am a good cook." So Seth showed the mole how to cook, and the mole showed Seth how to clean up. Seth and the mole are both happy now.

1. Seth's mother and father asked him to ____.

- leave home
- cook food
- cut down a tree

2. Who did Seth find living near a tree?

3. Who could cook well?

4. Who could clean up well?

5. Are Seth and the mole happy now?

13

ew
oi
aw
ar
dge
1. shadows
2. visiting
3. party
4. living
1. cheeks
2. smells
3. halls
4. friends
1. house
2. mouse
3. louder
4. shouting
1. chew
2. blew
3. news
1. toward
2. warn
3. through
4. kitchen
5. heard

Patty and the Cats
Part Two

Patty could not speak in a soft voice. But if you think her talking voice was loud, you should have heard her shouting voice. It was many times louder. That shouting voice was so loud that it shook the house. It made anybody near Patty have ringing ears.

One time, she was playing with some of her brothers and sisters. They started to tickle her, and she started to giggle. Then she started to laugh and shout. She shouted so loudly that she sent two of her sisters sailing into the air. Three of her brothers had such ringing in their ears that they did not hear well for six days.

That night, Patty was getting ready to go out with her family when her mom gave her some very bad news. “Patty,” her mom said. “You can’t go out with us tonight. It is just not safe.”

“Oh, please let me go,” Patty said. “I’ll be quiet. I won’t say a word.”

“I’m sorry,” her mom said. “You have to stay inside our home.”

Patty was very sad, but she did what her mom said. She watched the others go out. She felt big tears form in her eyes and run down her cheeks.

Patty's mom and dad were afraid because there were new smells in the house. Those were the smells of new cats. The mice didn't know it, but Arnold had four friends that were visiting him. They were large, nasty cats who loved to chase mice and pounce on them.

This is not the end.

Lesson 13

Jean and her brother did not know how to ride bikes. Jean's brother said, "I don't want to try to ride a bike." And he started to cry.

Jean said, "I do not know how to ride, but I will give it a good try." And she did.

Both Jean and her brother did not know how to read. Jean's brother cried, but Jean tried.

After a while, Jean could read and ride bikes. Jean's brother could not read or ride. Jean's brother was good at doing only one thing. He was good at crying.

1. Who tried to read?
2. Who didn't try?
3. At the end of the story, what could Jean do?
   - sit and cry
   - read and ride bikes
   - sing and play
4. Jean's brother was better than Jean at ______.

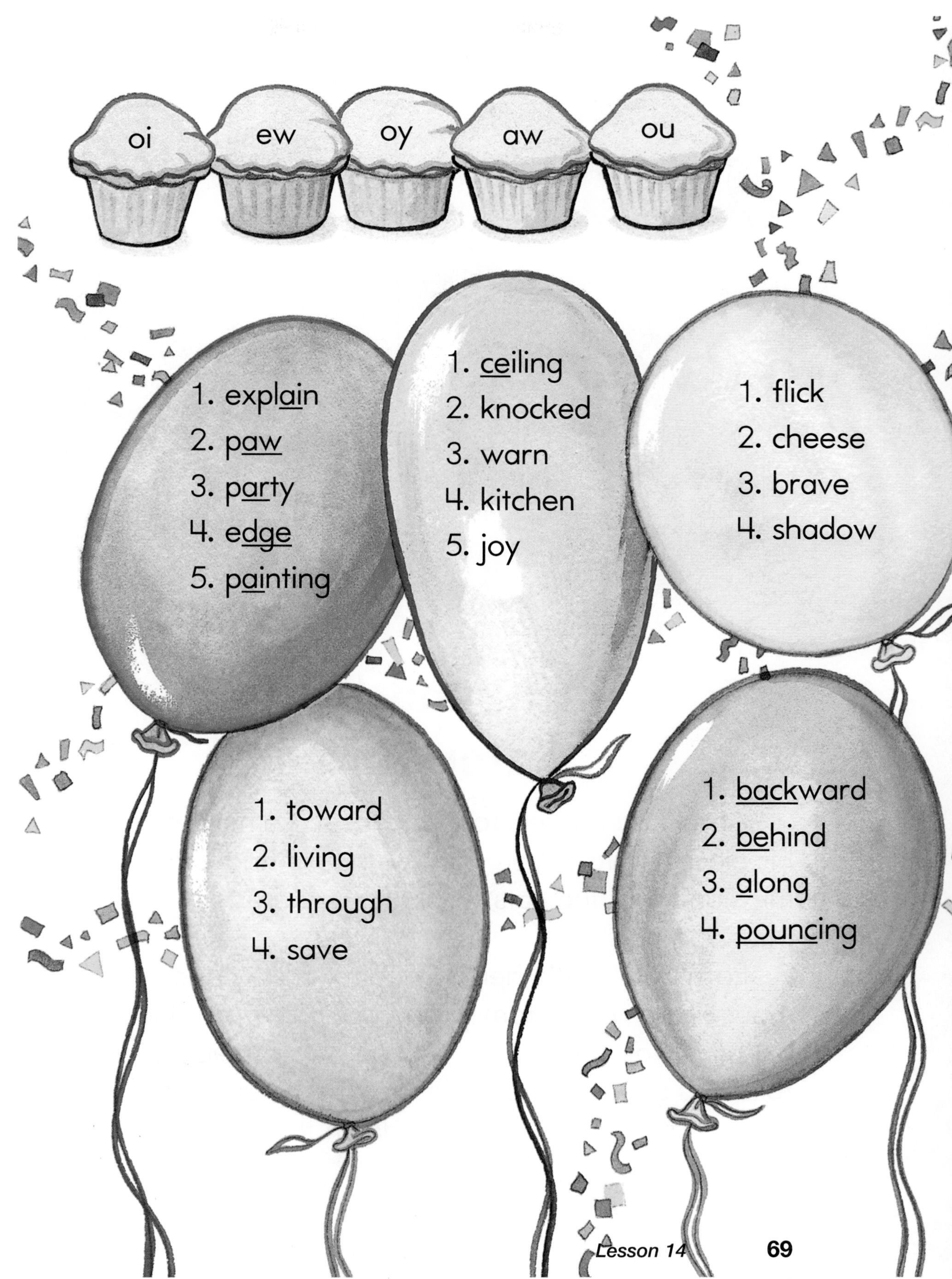
oi
ew
oy
aw
ou
1. explain
2. paw
3. party
4. edge
5. painting
1. ceiling
2. knocked
3. warn
4. kitchen
5. joy
1. flick
2. cheese
3. brave
4. shadow
1. toward
2. living
3. through
4. save
1. backward
2. behind
3. along
4. pouncing

Patty and the Cats
Part Three

Arnold had asked four friends to come over to his place. He told them that his house had lots of mice and that the cats would have a great pouncing party.

Patty was inside her home, looking out the mouse hole at her family. She could see her dad lead the way toward the kitchen. The others followed slowly along the edge of the rug in the living room. Then they snuck down the hall.

Suddenly, Patty saw something that gave her a great scare. It was the shadow of a cat, then another shadow and another. Three cats were following Patty's family into the kitchen.

Patty said to herself, "I must do something to save my family." Patty thought for a moment and then snuck through the mouse hole. She went along the edge of the rug and down the hall. She was now behind the three cats, and the three cats were behind Patty's family.

Patty was going to tell her family, "Cats are behind you. Run." But just as she was going to warn the others, she saw shadows on the other side of the kitchen. There were two more cats in front of Patty's family, waiting for them. If the mice started to run, they would run right into the cats who were waiting.

All five cats were slowly moving toward her family. One of the cats behind the mice was getting very close to one of Patty's sisters. That cat was getting ready to pounce.

More to come.

A goat named Gorman could not see well. One day, Gorman was walking in the field. He bumped into a scare crow. He said, "I'm sorry, I didn't see you standing there."

A crow was watching Gorman and said to herself, "I'll have some fun with Gorman."

The crow landed on top of the scare crow and said to Gorman, "Why don't you watch where you are going?"

Gorman said, "Well, I . . . I'm sorry. I'll be more careful next time."

A wise old snake saw what the crow was doing and slid over behind the crow. Then the snake said in a deep voice, "Oh, shame on you, crow, for playing tricks on that goat."

The crow took off and was never seen again.

1. What did Gorman bump into?
2. Did Gorman know that he bumped into a scare crow?
3. Who landed on top of the scare crow?
4. Who talked in a deep voice?
5. Did the snake scare the crow?

15

oy
ew
oi
or
aw
ce
1. high
2. tight
3. mirror
4. bounce
5. bonk
6. curled
7. noise
1. circus
2. through
3. ceiling
4. knocked
5. watching
1. trapeze
2. backward
3. behind
4. explained
5. loudest
1. cheese
2. brave
3. flick
4. joy
5. expert
1. paws
2. claws
3. blew
4. flew

Patty and the Cats Part Four

Patty's family was in the kitchen of the house. Behind them were three cats. In front of them were two more cats. One of the cats was getting ready to pounce on Patty's sister.

Patty tried to think, but her thoughts were mixed up. She just stood there in the dark, watching the cat flick his tail. Now the cat was starting to leap. Patty could see sharp claws on his front paws.

Without thinking, Patty shouted in her loudest voice, "WATCH OUT."

The room shook so hard that two paintings fell off the wall. One cat had planned to jump one foot high and land on Patty's sister. That cat jumped 8 feet high and hit his head against the ceiling. He landed on the kitchen table.

Patty's voice sent the other four cats flying, too. When those cats landed, they were howling and running as fast as they could go.

The mice had been knocked into a pile against the kitchen wall. Slowly they picked themselves up and went back to their mouse home with Patty.

When the mice were safe inside their home, Patty explained why she had shouted. Everybody in her family looked at her without saying a word. They didn't talk because they couldn't hear anything that Patty said.

Three days later, when the mice could hear again, they gave Patty a cheese party. Her dad said, "We are very proud of you. You are a brave mouse, and you saved us from those cats. Thank you."

Patty had tears in her eyes again. But they were tears of joy. From that day on, Patty went everywhere with her family. They didn't mind Patty's loud voice because they knew they would be safe.

The end.

A man woke up one night. He thought he heard a noise. He snuck from his bedroom into the dark hall. When he got to the end of the hall, he looked around the corner. He saw a face looking back at him. The man screamed and turned on the lights.

When the man looked around the corner again, he didn't see anyone. What he saw was a painting of himself hanging on the wall.

The man felt foolish. He said to himself, "I forgot that painting was there. I will remember that painting next time." Then he went back to sleep.

1. The man got up because he thought he heard ______.
   - a noise
   - a goat
   - Patty
2. The first time the man looked around the corner, what did he see?
   - a robber
   - a face
   - a dog
3. What did the man do?
   - ran
   - screamed
   - fainted
4. The man really saw a painting of ______.
5. Do you think the man will remember that painting next time?

16

1. liar
2. unicycle
3. yeah
4. argue
5. argument
6. known
1. tight
2. ad
3. noise
4. tent
5. riding
6. threw
1. circus
2. trapeze
3. juggle
4. settle
5. newspaper
6. perform
1. crowd
2. gather
3. Sherlock
4. Moe
5. nothing
6. expert

The Circus
Part One

Sherlock and Moe were known as the bragging rats. They did a lot of yelling, a lot of bragging, and a lot of lying.

A new fight started one spring day. Sherlock and Moe were looking at an ad that was on the ground. The ad was for a circus.

Moe said, "I can do circus tricks better than anybody else in the world. I can walk the tight rope. I can juggle anything. And I am an expert at riding a unicycle."

Sherlock said, "You think you're an expert. I am the expert. I can do tricks on the trapeze that you have never even seen before. I can juggle 12 nuts at once. I can . . . "

"That's nothing," Moe shouted. "I can juggle 40 nuts while I am on a trapeze doing tricks that nobody has ever seen before."

The rats shouted for a long time. The other rats in the pack were getting very tired of the noise and the lies. One of them was known as the wise old rat. He had a plan to make the bragging rats stop fighting.

The wise old rat walked over to the bragging rats and said, "Be quiet. There is a way to settle this. We will have a circus. And then we will see which of you does the best circus tricks."

So all the rats in the pack worked very hard to set up a circus tent with a tight rope, a trapeze, unicycles, and lots of things to juggle. Soon it was time for the bragging rats to show off their circus tricks.

More next time.

Winter was almost over, and Jan was sad. She loved to sled in the snow. She loved to hike in the snow. She just loved snow. But she knew that soon the snow would melt. She said to herself, "I will save some snow so I can have it later." She gathered up large piles of snow and took them to a place where the snow would not melt.

Later that day, Jan's mother came home from the store. She had food to put in the freezer. But when she opened up the freezer, she saw that there was no room for the food. The freezer was filled up with snow. Jan's mom was not very happy. And Jan had to take all that snow out of the freezer.

1. Jan was sad because winter was almost ______.

2. What did Jan love?

   • snow • rain • clouds

3. Where did Jan put her snow?

4. When her mom came home, was there room in the freezer?

5. What did Jan have to do with all the snow that was in the freezer?

ew
oy
oi
aw
ge
ce
1. tie
2. carry
3. closed
4. bounce
5. people
1. perform
2. expert
3. laughter
4. eaten
5. juggling
6. argue
1. eight
2. eye
3. heard
4. through
5. threw
6. asleep
1. climbed
2. ladder
3. answer
4. shoes
5. clown

The Circus Part Two

It was the day of the circus. Moe and Sherlock were still arguing. Moe said, "It's going to be so easy to beat you that I could do it with one eye closed and with one leg tied up."

"Oh yeah?" Sherlock said. "I could beat you while I was asleep with two legs tied up."

All the rats from the pack gathered in the tent. The wise old rat said, "Today we will have a contest of circus tricks. Behind me are the two rats who will perform. You will say which of the rats is the best at doing circus tricks."

The first contest was juggling. Moe started out with four nuts. He threw all four in the air. Two landed on his head. Two landed on the floor. None landed in his paws.

The crowd roared with laughter.

Sherlock started out with four nuts. He threw them into the air. Three nuts hit him on the head. One nut landed on the floor, bounced up, and landed in his paw. He said, "That is what I planned to do."

The crowd laughed.

The wise old rat said, "For the next contest, the rats will ride unicycles."

Both bragging rats tried to ride at the same time. They got on. They ran into each other. They fell down. And they did a lot of yelling at each other. "You knocked me down. Stay out of my way."

The crowd laughed a lot.

This story is not over.

One day, Henry said to himself, "I think I will go for a long walk." So he started to walk. He walked from his house to the other side of town. When he got there, he said, "I think I'll just keep on walking." And that's what he did. He walked all day long. At the end of the day, he said, "I don't want to walk any more." So he stopped right where he was.

He was next to a farm house. After a while, the farmer came out and said, "Why don't you go back home?"

Henry said, "Because I don't want to walk any more."

The farmer said, "Well, then, why don't you run home?"

Henry liked that plan. So he ran home.

1. One day, Henry went for a long ______.

2. Did he stop walking when he got to the other side of town?

3. When he finally stopped, he was near a ______.

4. Did he want to walk any more?

5. So how did he get home?

18

ew aw oy oi ou
1. change
2. east
3. west
4. porch
5. few
1. ladder
2. ouch
3. night
4. snooze
5. yawn
6. flew
7. crawl
1. tightly
2. climbing
3. crawling
4. polite
5. noisy
1. violin
2. sure
3. school
4. shoes
1. won
2. spite
3. amaze
4. clown
5. vote

The Circus
Part Three

After the bragging rats tried to juggle and ride unicycles, they tried walking the tight rope.

Moe climbed the ladder and was getting ready to go on the tight rope. He looked scared. Then he said, "Oh, I forgot my tight rope shoes. So I can't do it."

As Moe started back down the ladder, he slipped and fell. The crowd laughed.

Sherlock said, "You don't even know how to walk on a tight rope. Watch me."

He climbed the ladder and crawled out on the tight rope. Then he slipped and was hanging by one paw. Then he was yelling and hanging by no paws. Ouch. He landed on the floor, and the crowd laughed.

The last contest was the trapeze. Both the rats tried to get on the same trapeze, but soon both of them were hanging by one paw. Then they were hanging by no paws. Ouch.

The rats in the crowd laughed so loudly that they could not hear the bragging rats yelling at each other. "You got in my way. I was getting ready to do a great trick."

"No, you got in my way."

After the laughter stopped, everyone voted for the rat that did the best circus tricks.

Did one of the bragging rats win the juggling contest or the unicycle contest? No.

Did one of them win the tight rope contest or the trapeze contest? No.

But all the other rats agreed that the bragging rats won one contest. They were the best clowns anybody had ever seen.

"I know that," Moe said. "Because I'm the best clown in the world."

"No way," Sherlock said. "I got a lot more laughter than you did. People who know good clowns know I am really funny."

The wise old rat said, "More arguing. Here we go again."

This story is over.

A boy loved things that flew. He loved airplanes and birds and kites and balloons. He asked his mother, "Could I be a bird so I can fly?"

His mother said, "You can not be a bird. You are a boy, and boys can't be birds."

The boy said, "But I want to fly."

"You can't fly," his mother said. "But you can fly your kite."

The boy thought flying his kite was a great plan. So he and his mother went to the park and flew his kite.

1. The boy loved things that ______.

2. The boy asked his mother if he could be a ______.

3. She told him to fly a ______.

4. Where did the boy and his mother go to fly a kite?

1. pledge
2. bridge
3. change
4. space
5. dice

1. package
2. milking
3. understand
4. clothespin
5. violin
6. letters
7. summer
8. wasn't

1. Goober
2. porch
3. snooze
4. chew
5. few
6. threw

1. closed
2. beet
3. dot
4. west
5. squeak
6. east

Goober
Part One

There once were two towns, East Town and West Town. Those towns were about two miles apart. Right between the two towns was a farm. And on that farm lived a man everybody called Goober.

That wasn't really his name, but that's what they called him. Everybody knew Goober. If you asked the people who lived in East Town or West Town what they thought about Goober, you would find out that they didn't know how to feel about him. They liked him for some things, and they hated him for other things.

They liked his music. It was sweet and fine. Goober made music with an old violin. You would never know it was old from the lovely sound it made. Goober sat on his porch every summer evening and played his violin. The air would carry that music for miles.

So the people in East Town and West Town would sit outside and listen to the sweet music if the wind was blowing the right way.

But if the wind was not blowing the right way, most people didn't stay outside and listen to the music. They ran inside very fast. And at those times, most people didn't like Goober. Why? Goober's farm had a very bad smell. He had dirty pigs that never took a bath. And their smell was so bad that when the wind was blowing to the east, people in East Town could smell it. Most people would say "phew" and go inside. They would close all the doors and windows—even if the evening was very warm. They would keep their houses closed up until the wind changed and stopped blowing toward East Town.

A few people would stay outside and listen to the music. Those people would put a clothespin over their nose so they could not smell anything. They would listen to the music until after the sun went down. Then they would go inside and take the clothespin off their nose.

More to come.

A dog loved to dig. He found a little mole hole and started to make it bigger. And as the hole got deeper and deeper, the hill of dirt next to the hole got bigger and bigger. Soon that hill was almost as big as a mountain. The dog told his pals, "I made a mountain out of a mole hill."

A mole saw the mountain and said, "This pile of dirt is too big." So the mole started putting the dirt back into the hole. The mountain got smaller and smaller until it was a tiny hill. The mole told his pals, "The dog made a mountain out of a mole hill, but I made a mole hill out of a mountain."

1. Who made a mole hole bigger?
2. The dog told his pals that he made a ______ out of a ______.
3. Who put most of the dirt back in the hole?
4. The mole told his pals that he made a ______ out of a ______.

20

A

1. bulldog
2. butterflies
3. snowflakes
4. clothespin
5. package
6. understand

B

1. danger
2. dice
3. lodge
4. golly
5. south
6. stink

C

1. milking
2. holding
3. scrubbed
4. cleaned
5. smelling
6. sniffed

D

1. catch
2. lost
3. track
4. bone
5. letters

E

1. different
2. soap
3. wash
4. crawl

Goober
Part Two

Goober lived on a farm that was right between two towns. When the wind was blowing to the east, most of the people in East Town were not very happy. And when the wind was blowing to the west, most of the people in West Town were not very happy.

The people were not happy because of the smell from Goober's farm. But when they ran inside to get away from the smell, they could not hear the sweet music. Some people really wanted to hear the music. Those people stayed outside and put a clothespin on their nose. But then they didn't like to talk to each other. They couldn't say words that had the letters **N** or **M.** They couldn't say the word **not.** It sounded like **dot.** They couldn't say the word **meet.** It sounded like **beet.**

The people in East Town and West Town loved it when there was no wind. Then they could all sit outside and listen to Goober's lovely violin music. Some people liked Goober all the time. They lived more than a mile from Goober's farm. The wind would carry the smell from Goober's pigs a mile, but no more. So the smell would not reach people who lived far away. They could listen to the sweet music without having to smell Goober's farm.

Then one summer morning, something very strange happened. A little girl from West Town went over to Goober's farm to visit him. That was strange because nobody ever visited Goober.

The little girl took a big package with her. She walked up to his barn. Goober was milking a cow. Stinky pigs were all around him. The little girl held her nose because the smell was very bad. She tried to say, "Mister Goober, you make nice music."

But she was holding her nose. So here is how it sounded. "Bister Goober, you bake dice busic."

Goober looked up and said, "I do what?"

She said, "Bake dice busic."

He said, "I don't understand. If you would stop holding your nose, I would know what you are trying to say."

More to come.

Kathy liked to go to the forest and look for birds. One day she went into the forest and heard a little tiny bird song. She said to herself, "That bird has a tiny voice, so it must be a tiny bird." She looked up in the trees and saw a tiny yellow bird.

Then she heard a great loud bird song. She said to herself, "That must be a great big bird." She looked up in the trees and all around, but she did not see a great big bird. She saw some black birds and a little tiny red bird. As she was watching the red bird, it opened its little tiny beak and let out a great loud song. Kathy said to herself, "Some birds have a little body, but a big voice."

1. Where did Kathy go to see birds?
2. One day she heard a tiny song and saw a ______ yellow bird.
3. What kind of song did she hear next?
4. Was a big bird or a little bird making that song?
5. What kind of voice do some tiny birds have?

1. stink
2. scrubbed
3. sniffed
4. strange
5. stream

1. waddle
2. middle
3. bulldog
4. yawning
5. shocked

1. poor
2. gone
3. wrong
4. hours
5. flat
6. south

1. life
2. track
3. ham
4. bone
5. rabbit
6. golly
7. different

Goober
Part Three

A little girl went to visit Goober. She had a package with her. She tried to talk to Goober, but she was holding her nose, and he could not understand what she was trying to say. She tried to say, "You make nice music," but she really said, "You bake dice busic." Goober told her to stop holding her nose so he could understand what she was saying.

So the little girl took in a lot of air. Then she let go of her nose and talked very quickly. She said, "We love your music, but you need to clean up your pigs. They stink." When she was done talking, she grabbed her nose again.

Goober's eyes got wide. He looked at the little girl for a long time. Then he said, "Do my pigs really stink?"

She said, "Yes."

"Golly," he said. "I didn't know that."

She handed Goober her package and said, "Here are sub thigs for you." She turned around and ran away. She was still holding her nose.

Goober opened the package. Inside were some bars of pig soap.

Goober smelled the soap and said, "What a strange smell."

Then Goober went down to the pond with the package. He called his pigs. They came running. Then he jumped into the pond with the pigs and scrubbed them until they were pink. Scrub, scrub, scrub. He rubbed and scrubbed and washed and cleaned. When he was done, his pigs were as clean and sweet smelling as anybody in East Town or West Town. He sniffed the air and said, "Those pigs really smell strange."

Now things are different in West Town and East Town. People sit outside and listen to the music every summer evening. And the air is as sweet as the violin music they listen to. If you go to one of those towns and ask people about Goober, they'll have wonderful things to say about him and his music. And they also have some very nice things to say about a little girl from West Town who goes to visit Goober every week. She always leaves a package with him, and the people in West Town and East Town are very glad that she does.

The end.

Marta didn't like to get dirty, but she wanted to help her mom plant some trees in their yard. She put on her mittens so her hands wouldn't get dirty. She put on her old pants, too. She didn't want to get her nice school pants dirty.

Marta's mom was very dirty from planting trees in the dirt. Her hands were dirty, and her shirt was dirty. There was dirt even in her hair.

Marta went outside to help her mom plant the trees. They watered the plants and patted the dirt around the plants. Marta got mud all over her mittens. When she rubbed her face, she got dirt on her face. Pretty soon, Marta had dirt on her shirt and dirt on her pants. Soon she was as dirty as her mom. But Marta didn't mind. She told her mom, "Sometimes getting dirty is fun."

1. What did Marta want to help her mom do?
2. Marta put on mittens to keep her hands from getting ____.
3. Did Marta's mom get dirty?
4. Did Marta get dirty?
5. She said, "Sometimes getting dirty is ____."

22

aw
ew
oi
ce
dge
1. Andrea
2. Honey
3. Sweetie
4. waddle
5. life
6. middle
7. butterflies
1. lesson
2. alarm
3. napping
4. swung
5. hissed
6. net
7. snort
1. nip
2. snip
3. flew
4. threw
1. ski
2. interesting
3. cloth
4. often
5. station

Honey and Sweetie
Part One

There once was the meanest looking bulldog you ever saw. Her bottom teeth stuck out, and she looked like she was ready to bite somebody. People were always shocked to find out that this bulldog was named Honey.

She got that name because she was as sweet as honey. She loved people. She loved other dogs. She even liked some animals you would not think a dog would like. One of Honey's friends was a little gray mouse named Andrea.

Honey would sometimes sniff around the house trying to find Andrea. Andrea lived in the hall. She really lived behind a little hole in the hall wall. But in the middle of the day, she could be in a lot of places. So Honey would sniff around and try to find her. Sometimes Honey would find Andrea, and sometimes she wouldn't, because Andrea was very, very shy.

There was only one thing that Honey didn't like. That was cats. She could get along with some cats. But she really didn't like cats that chased birds, butterflies, or mice. She said to herself, "That's not nice."

One day, Honey was napping on the back porch of her house. She woke up when a woman holding a big yellow cat came up the steps. When Honey saw that cat, she said to herself, "Yuk. I hope that thing does not stay around here very long."

The woman and the cat went inside. After a while, Honey got up, yawned, and waddled into the house.

The woman was sitting at the table, but where was the cat? That's what the woman wanted to know, too. She said, "Where did Sweetie go?"

Everybody found out where he was in the next moment. The sounds of running came from the next room. Honey waddled into that room. Then she became very mad. She saw poor little Andrea running for her life. And right behind her was that mean yellow cat. The cat and the mouse shot around the room, this way and that way. They went under the table and across the rug. Then they went into the hall, around a coat stand, and back to the room where Honey was standing.

More next time.

Sammy the goat liked to go for walks. He would walk around the farm every day. He walked around for a very long time. Sammy never got tired of walking.

One day, Sammy wanted to walk to the forest. That forest was very far away. He told the other goats, "I'm going to walk all the way to the forest, and I'm going alone."

"No, don't go alone," the other goats said. "It's too far."

Sammy didn't listen to those goats. So he walked for miles and miles. Pretty soon, it was getting dark, and Sammy still wasn't at the forest. He was starting to get scared.

This is not the end.

1. What did Sammy like to do?
2. Where did Sammy want to walk to?
3. Was the forest near the farm?
4. Did his goat friends think he should go alone?
5. It was getting dark, and Sammy was starting to get ______.

A

1. ski
2. cloth
3. often
4. station
5. waddled

B

1. scraps
2. thick
3. nip
4. hissed
5. howled
6. given

D

1. interesting
2. kennel
3. snorting
4. sticking
5. lesson

C

1. soup
2. slopes
3. ruff
4. meat
5. net
6. swung

E

1. problem
2. hurt
3. ranger
4. weak

Honey and Sweetie
Part Two

Poor little Andrea was being chased by a mean yellow cat named Sweetie. They had run down the hall and back into the room where Honey was standing. Honey was ready to help Andrea out, but before she could do anything, Andrea and Sweetie darted under the table. Sweetie tried to pounce on Andrea, but his claws got stuck on the table cloth. Down came the table cloth. It fell over Sweetie like a big white net.

Sweetie tried to get free. He swung at the table cloth, bit at it, and tried to roll away from it. But the more he tried to fight and roll, the more he was trapped inside that table cloth. Only two parts of Sweetie were sticking out. His yellow tail was sticking out of one end of the table cloth, and his nose was sticking out of the other end.

While Sweetie was rolling around and trying to get free, Andrea darted down the hall and into her hole. She was very scared. Honey looked at Sweetie and said to herself, "It is time to teach this cat a lesson."

She waddled over to Sweetie and gave his tail a little bite. It was not a great bite, just a little nip. "There," Honey said to herself, and waddled outside.

Sweetie howled and hissed and rolled around inside the table cloth. At last, he got free. He looked around the room, but he didn't see Andrea because she was in her mouse hole. And Sweetie didn't see Honey because she was outside. Sweetie didn't know who bit his tail. He never saw Honey in the room, so he didn't even think about her. He said to himself, "The only one who could have given me that big bite was that little tiny mouse."

Sweetie shook his head and said to himself, "That mouse looks really weak, but she can really bite hard."

That was the last time Sweetie ever chased Andrea. In fact, there are a lot of things that Sweetie does not chase. He doesn't chase mice, and he doesn't even chase little birds.

The end.

Sammy had been walking for a very long time, and it was getting dark. Sammy was scared to be alone in the dark. He stopped near a stream and said, "I wish my friends were here." Then he said, "I will rest here. I hope no lions or tigers come after me."

Just as he was falling asleep, he heard loud noises. Somebody was coming closer and closer. Sammy was very scared. But just then, he saw who was coming. It was his goat friends. One of them shouted, "Sammy, we couldn't let you go by yourself. We wanted to make sure you were safe."

The next day, Sammy and his pals walked to the forest together.

The end.

1. Sammy was scared to be alone in the ______.
2. Where did Sammy stop and rest?
3. What did he hear in the dark?
4. Who went with him to the forest the next day?

24

1. often
2. gone
3. wrong
4. lost

1. hours
2. catch
3. alarm
4. snorting

1. chasing
2. finding
3. tracking
4. picking
5. acting
6. ranger
7. higher

1. climbers
2. snowballs
3. rabbit
4. danger

1. Dud
2. ham
3. slope
4. flat

Dot and Dud
Part One

Once there were two big work dogs named Dot and Dud. Dot was Dud's sister. The two dogs lived with five other work dogs at the ranger station high in the mountains. Their job was to find mountain climbers who got lost or hurt. That was their job, but there was one big problem with that job. That problem was Dud. They called him Dud because that's what he was—a big dud at doing his job. When a climber was missing, the ranger would send the dogs to find him. The other dogs would find the climber. Then they would have to find Dud. Dud would get lost. Most of the time, the dog who found the mountain climber was Dot. She was the best dog in all the mountains.

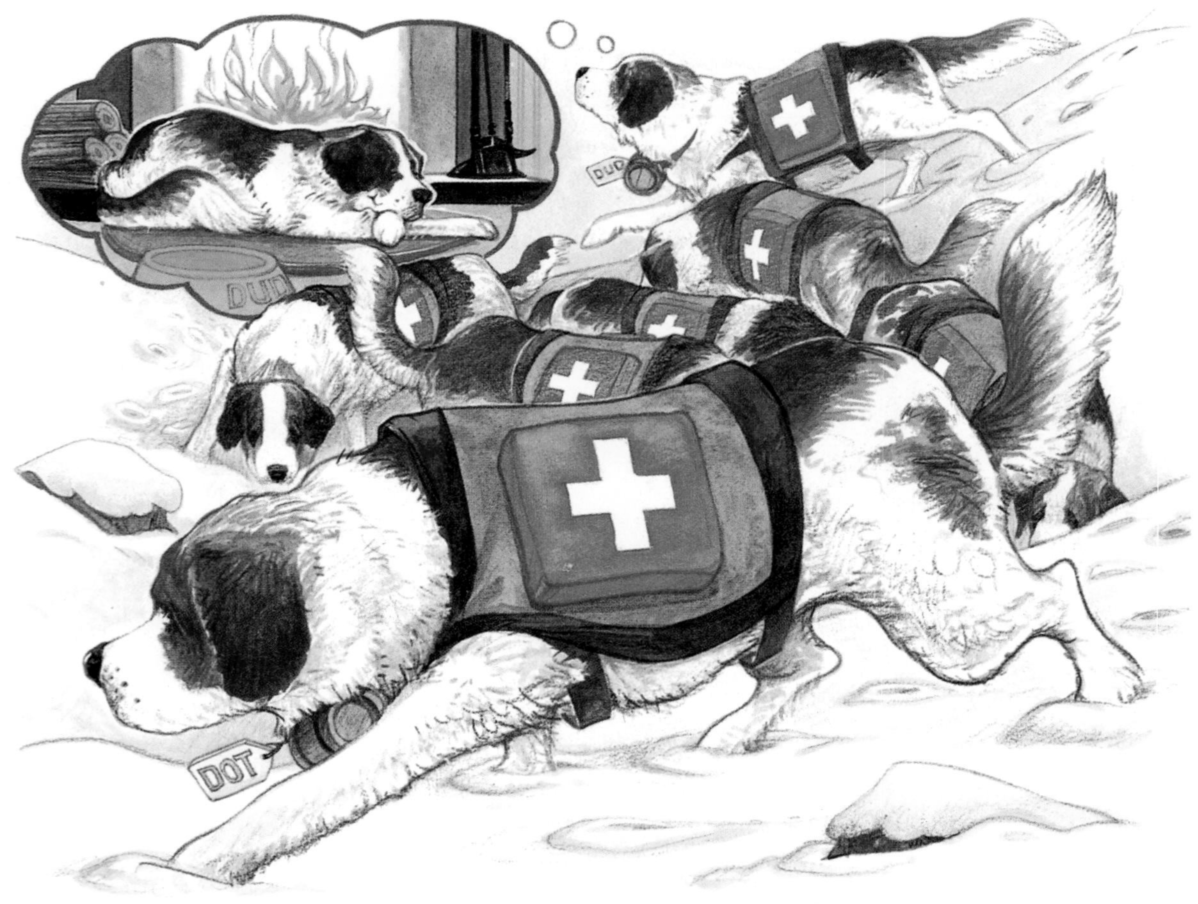

Dud was not good at his job because he didn't like to work. He didn't like to put his nose in the cold snow and sniff for a smell that would lead him to the lost climber. Dud acted like he was tracking through the snow, but he was just acting. While he should have been thinking about finding the lost climber, he was often thinking about eating a large ham bone or sleeping next to the big fire place down at the ranger's station.

Most of the other work dogs would get mad at Dud because they knew he wasn't trying hard. "Come on," they'd say to him. "Stop being such a baby and get to work."

"Okay," Dud would say. "I will. I will." But he didn't.

One time, the other dogs got really mad. Dud had gone out to find a climber, but he got lost. The other dogs spent hours finding him. When they got back to the kennel, the oldest dog said, "While we work, you are out there playing around, running after your tail, rolling snowballs with your nose, or chasing rabbits."

"Yeah," another dog said. "And you don't even know where you are. When we found you, you were less than a mile from the station, and you didn't even know how to get back here."

Dot said, "Stop picking on my brother. He can do this job, and he will work hard. Won't you, Dud?"

"I will. I will," Dud said. "I'll work hard."

Dud was not telling a lie. He had made up his mind to do a good job. But of course, the other dogs didn't believe him.

More next time.

He'll work hard.
No, he won't.
DOT
DUD
I will. I will.

A black eagle lived near a stream. One day that eagle was in a tree when she saw a big fish. She said, "That fish is near a brown rock. So I will swoop down and go right over that rock. Then I will grab that fish."

The eagle swooped down, but her plan didn't work, because the brown rock moved. And she flew right into it. That brown rock was not a rock at all. It was a moose. And the moose was very mad at the eagle.

So now the eagle makes sure there are no big brown rocks in the stream before she swoops down to go fishing.

1. Who wanted to get a fish?

2. Was the eagle red, yellow, or black?

3. The eagle planned to swoop over a ______.

4. What was the brown rock?

5. Was the moose happy or mad?

25

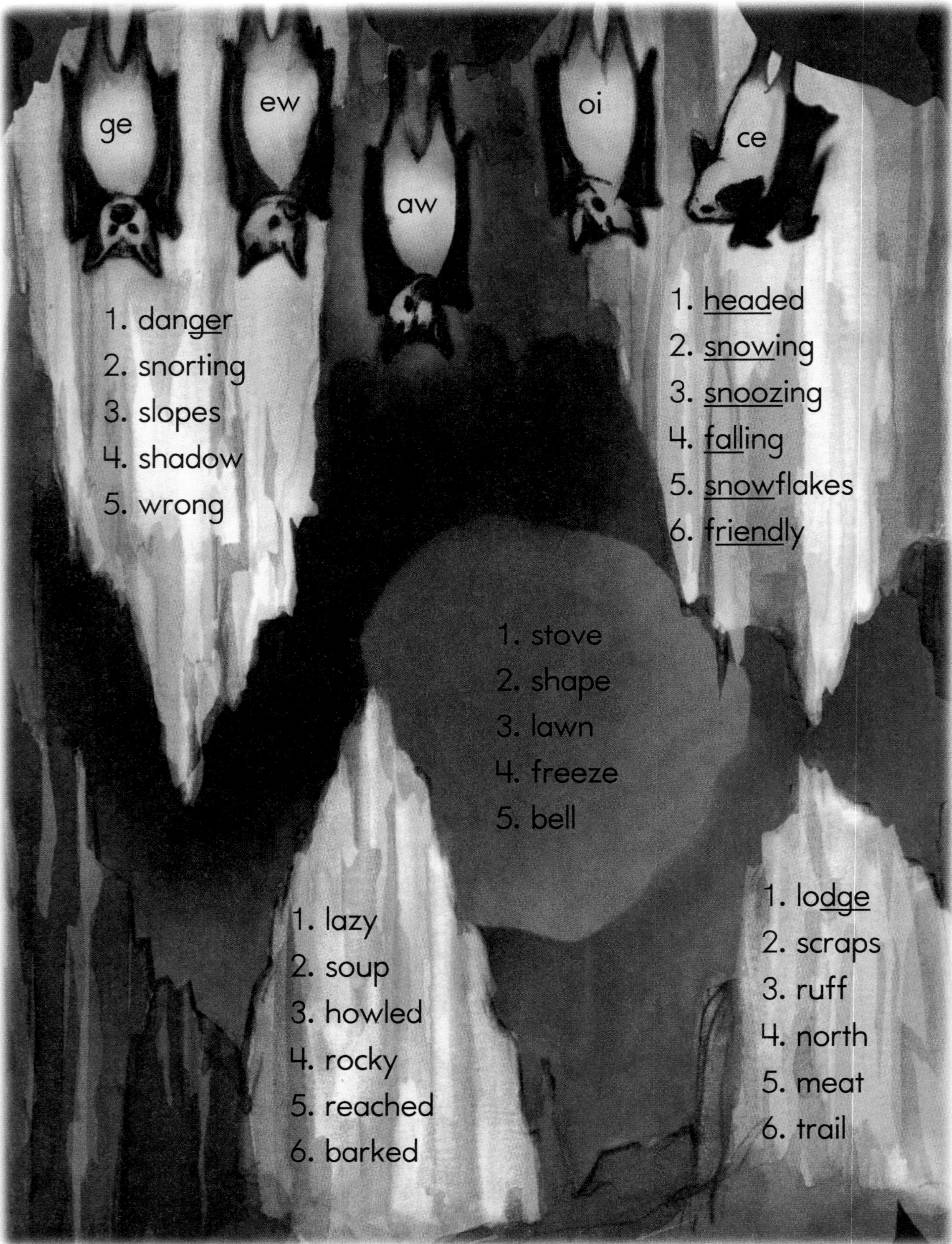
ge
ew
aw
oi
ce
1. danger
2. snorting
3. slopes
4. shadow
5. wrong
1. headed
2. snowing
3. snoozing
4. falling
5. snowflakes
6. friendly
1. stove
2. shape
3. lawn
4. freeze
5. bell
1. lazy
2. soup
3. howled
4. rocky
5. reached
6. barked
1. lodge
2. scraps
3. ruff
4. north
5. meat
6. trail

Dot and Dud
Part Two

The other work dogs were mad at Dud for being a dud. Dud was also mad at himself. He had made up his mind to try harder. That's what he told the others, but they didn't believe him. He had said the same thing many times before.

Just then, the alarm sounded. That told the dogs that a mountain climber was in danger. Three rangers ran to the kennel and let the dogs out. They all headed north to where mountain climbers climb. The dogs sniffed for the trail of the lost climber as they went up higher and higher. Dud even put his nose in the snow a few times and tried very hard to smell something. It was hard work, sniffing and snorting and going up the steep slope.

After a while, Dud began to walk slower and slower. Soon he was far behind the other dogs. Then Dud came to a place that was not steep. It was almost flat. There, Dud did something that was more interesting than sniffing snow. He chased his shadow. Dud jumped up, and the shadow moved. Dud pounced on the shadow. He rolled over on the shadow. He ran around and around, faster and faster, trying to catch that shadow. He even barked at his shadow. This was fun, fun, fun.

Right in the middle of the game, the shadow went away. Dud looked up and saw clouds in the sky. Now it was snowing. Dud couldn't see any of the other dogs. He knew that they were heading north, but he had been running around so much that he didn't know which way north was. He knew that he had to go up a slope, but there were a lot of slopes. Which slope was the right one?

Soon the snow was coming down so hard that Dud couldn't see any slopes—only snow, snow, snow.

Dud looked this way and that way. He tried to sniff the air, but all he could smell were snowflakes. At last he made a choice about which way to go, and his choice was wrong, wrong, wrong. Poor Dud started heading south, not north. He was heading right back toward the ranger station.

More next time.

Little Billy loved to go shopping. One day he said, "Today, I'm going to go shopping for more than I ever shopped for." So Billy went to the big store in the mall. That store had everything. Little Billy got a cart and loaded it with shoes, coats, tools, food, books, and just about anything else he could reach. Then Billy started to take his things out of the store. A big man stopped him and said, "You have to pay for these things."

Little Billy looked up at the man and said, "Pay? I don't know how to pay."

Just then Billy's mom ran into the store. She said, "I'm sorry for what happened. Little Billy sometimes forgets that he is just three years old."

1. What did Billy like to do?

2. Name two things he put in his cart.

3. Billy had to ▬ ▬ the things before he could take them out of the store.

4. What kind of man stopped Billy?

5. How old was Billy?

1. hadn't
2. where's
3. who's
4. there's
1. stove
2. shape
3. know
4. knew
5. curled
6. waited
1. station
2. bother
3. brother
4. lazy
5. warm
1. early
2. notice
3. cook
4. puppies
5. dreaming
6. remembered
7. snowy

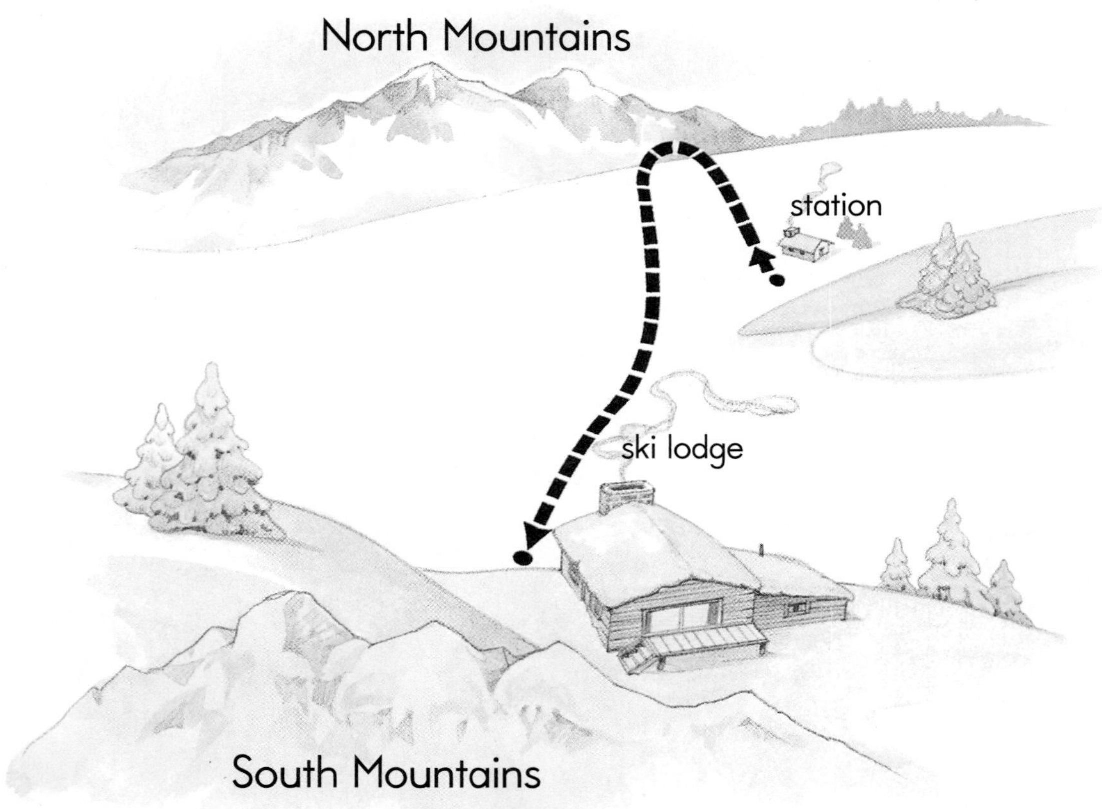

Dud and Dot
Part Three

Dud was trying to go north, but he went south. He went very close to the ranger station. But he didn't see it and went right on past it. The snow was coming down so hard that he couldn't see the station, and he was so lazy that he didn't bother sniffing with his nose. So Dud passed up that station and went up a mountain to the south of the station. At last he came to a large ski lodge where there were many people.

Dud did not know where he was, but he said to himself, “There are people here, so there must be a kitchen around here.” Dud found the kitchen very quickly by sniffing for the smells of ham and eggs.

Then Dud put on a little act. He sat outside the kitchen and made little barks. “Ruff, ruff.” When a woman opened the door, he wagged his tail and tried to look very friendly, but also very cold.

“What are you doing out here?” the woman said. “You poor dog. You must be very hungry and tired. Come in here.”

She led Dud inside and gave him a lot of soup and a big pile of meat scraps. This was like a dream for Dud. He ate everything and then took a wonderful nap right next to the big, warm stove. He was one happy dog.

But while he was snoozing, things were not going well for the other dogs. Dot had found the trail of the lost mountain climber, but in the snow storm, the other dogs could not keep up with her. She followed the trail up slopes that were so steep that she kept slipping. Once she slipped and slid down a long way. Dot got up and kept trying until she reached a rocky place where the mountain climber was sitting. He was hurt and couldn't walk. He just sat there with his eyes closed. Dot knew that he was in bad shape.

She barked and howled as loud as she could, but the sound of her barks did not go far in the thick falling snow. The other dogs were over a mile away, and they did not hear anything. Dot didn't know what to do, so she curled up next to the mountain climber to keep him warm. Then she waited, and waited, and waited. It was getting close to night time.

More to come.

DUD
DOT
I hope they find us soon.

Not all fish in the sea look the same. You can tell where a fish lives by the shape of the fish. Fish that live near the shore are shaped like this.  The shape of these fish lets them turn quickly.

Fish that live in the open water look like this. 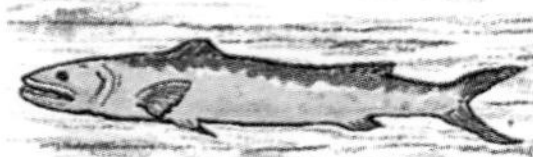 The shape of these fish lets them go very fast.

Some fish that live in the open water hunt other fish. They have to be fast. Sometimes they come near the shore and hunt fish shaped like this. 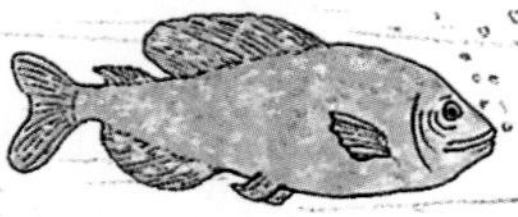 The fish near the shore are good at getting away from the hunting fish.

1. Do all fish that live in the sea have the same shape?
2. Where do fish with this  shape live?
3. Where do fish with this  shape live?
4. Which fish can turn quickly, fish that live near the shore or fish that live in the open water?
5. Which fish can swim very fast?

1. tomorrow
2. practice
3. finish
4. somewhere
1. station
2. nation
3. question
4. action
5. motion
1. right
2. slight
3. quietly
4. quickly
5. cook
1. early
2. knowing
3. noticed
4. puppies
5. snowy
6. plowing

Dot and Dud
Part Four

That evening, while Dud was sleeping in the kitchen and dreaming of summer time, a truck pulled up to the ski lodge. The head ranger came inside to pick up Dud. The cook had called the ranger station and told them that one of their dogs was at the lodge.

The ranger was not happy. He led Dud to the truck and put him in the back with the other work dogs. They were coming back from the north mountains. They had not found the mountain climber, and they hadn't found Dot. The ranger wanted to come home before it got too dark. He planned to go out again early in the morning.

When Dud got in the truck, he didn't know that Dot was somewhere on the mountain. But right away, he knew that something was wrong. The other dogs didn't start complaining about Dud getting lost. Those dogs didn't even look at him. They just looked down at the floor.

Dud tried to talk to the other dogs. “Did you find the mountain climber?” he asked. The other dogs didn’t say a thing. They just looked down.

Dud said, “You know, I had some wonderful soup at the ski lodge, and I . . .”

“Be quiet,” the oldest dog said.

Dud was quiet for a while. Then he noticed that Dot was not in the truck. “Where’s Dot?” he asked.

“Lost,” one of the work dogs said.

“What do you mean?” Dud asked. “Where is she?”

“Somewhere on the mountain,” the oldest dog said.

“Do you mean she’s out there alone?”

Some of the dogs said, “Yes,” very quietly.

Dud loved Dot. He didn't always show it, but he loved her. As he sat in the back of that truck, he remembered her from way back, when Dot and Dud were little puppies. When any other puppy would pick on Dud, Dot always stuck up for him. Dud remembered a lot of other things as the truck went down that snowy road. He remembered how sad he had been when he and Dot had to leave their mother. The only good thing about going to the ranger station was that Dot was with him.

More to come.

Once there was a rabbit who always bragged about how fast she was. One day, when the rabbit was bragging, a little mole said, "I will race you."

The rabbit laughed and laughed. "I will race you anytime," the rabbit said.

"Fine," the mole said. "Be here at one o'clock at night. And if you do not win the race, you will stop bragging."

The rabbit agreed.

That night, the rabbit and the mole were ready to start the race. Many other animals were there to watch the race, too, but it was so dark that most of the animals couldn't see. The mole said, "Ready, set, go," and both animals started to run.

Did the rabbit win the race? No. She didn't even finish the race, because she couldn't see. She ran into a rock. She heard bells and saw stars. Now she doesn't brag. She thinks she's a mole named Bill.

1. What kind of animal bragged?

2. Who said he would race the rabbit?

3. When did the race start?

4. Why didn't the rabbit win?

5. Now the rabbit thinks she is a ______.

28

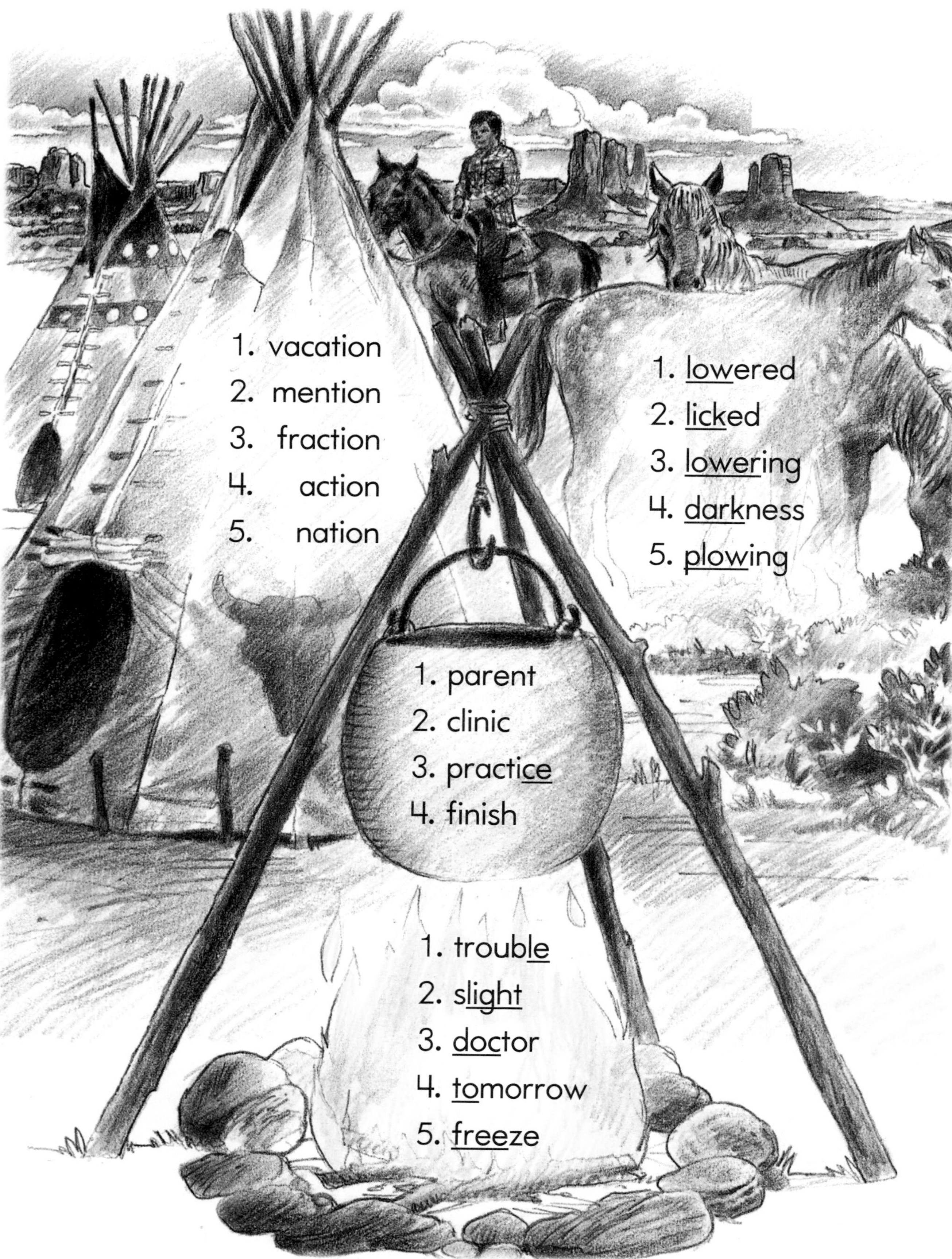
1. vacation
2. mention
3. fraction
4. action
5. nation
1. lowered
2. licked
3. lowering
4. darkness
5. plowing
1. parent
2. clinic
3. practice
4. finish
1. trouble
2. slight
3. doctor
4. tomorrow
5. freeze

Dot and Dud
Part Five

Dud was in the back of the ranger's truck, remembering how much he loved Dot. All at once, he said, "No, she can't be lost." Then he turned to the oldest dog and asked, "Why did you leave her out there?"

"She'll be all right, if we find her early in the morning."

Dud said, "But what about the mountain climber? Won't he freeze if he stays out there much longer?"

All the other dogs looked down.

Dud didn't say anything more to the other dogs. But he said something to himself. He said, "If they can't find her, I'll find her." Dud was not talking the way he sometimes did when he said, "I'll be better." This was not a game.

The truck stopped in front of the ranger station. As soon as the ranger opened the back door, Dud jumped out and ran as fast as he could. The ranger shouted, "Dud, come back here. It's dark out there."

The other dogs barked and yelled at him. Dud knew where he was going—north.

Pretty soon some of the other dogs started to follow Dud. Then all of them followed. Then the ranger followed. Away they went, plowing through the deep snow up the mountain. Dud said to himself, "I know Dot's smell better than anyone else's in the world. I will find that smell. I will. I will."

He put his nose in the snow and snorted and sniffed. He didn't even notice that the snow was cold. Again and again—snort, sniff, snort, sniff. Then he did it the fast way. He just put his nose in the snow and kept it there, like a snow plow, snorting and sniffing. And up the mountain he went, just as fast as he could run.

Suddenly, there was a very slight smell in the snow. It was Dot. Yes, yes, yes. It was Dot. "Come on," he barked to the other dogs. "Follow me."

And up the mountain he went once more, his head in the snow like a snow plow. When he came to steep parts and slid down, he just tried harder and did it again until he made it. Her smell was getting stronger and stronger.

More to come.

Jim was a snake that loved to eat bugs. He could eat and eat and eat. One year, there were lots of bugs, and Jim ate, and ate, and ate. But the more he ate, the fatter he got. Soon he was so fat that he could not sneak up on bugs. He wouldn't slide through the grass. He would plow through the grass. All the bugs would hear him coming. They would call to each other and say, "Here comes that fat snake again. Let's get out of here."

And they would.

Right now, Jim has not had a bug to eat in two weeks. He is not as fat as he was. He can slide through the grass better than he did before. But he is still too slow. He won't catch any bugs for another week. By then, he'll be a slim Jim.

1. What kind of animal is Jim?
2. What did he love to eat?
3. One year, there were a lot of ______.
4. What happened to Jim after he ate and ate?
5. Could he sneak up on bugs any more?
6. How long will it be before he is a slim Jim?

29

ew oy tion aw

1. direct
2. direc<u>tion</u>
3. inform
4. informa<u>tion</u>
5. collect
6. collec<u>tion</u>

1. <u>bor</u>ing
2. <u>snor</u>ing
3. <u>will</u>ing
4. <u>high</u>er
5. <u>strong</u>er
6. <u>dark</u>ness

1. minutes
2. popular
3. either
4. except
5. wife

1. through
2. thought
3. lawn
4. curled
5. lowered
6. doctor

Dot and Dud
Part Six

Dud was leading the other dogs high into the mountains. He knew that he was getting very close to Dot because her smell was strong.

Suddenly Dud stopped and looked up. He had come to the rocky part where Dot was curled up next to the mountain climber. For a moment, Dud stood there and looked into the darkness. He could see Dot. He ran over, sat down next to her, and licked her nose. “Are you okay?” he asked.

“Yes,” she said. “But I’m so glad you’re here. I don’t think the mountain climber can make it through the night.”

Dot and Dud looked at each other and wagged their tails. Then Dud called to the other dogs, “Come up here. I found them.”

In a little while, the ranger and the other dogs made it up the steep slope. The ranger had a little sled. He put the climber on the sled. He and the dogs lowered the sled down the steep slope. Then the dogs pulled the sled back to the ranger station.

After the ranger put the dogs in the kennel, he took the mountain climber to a doctor.

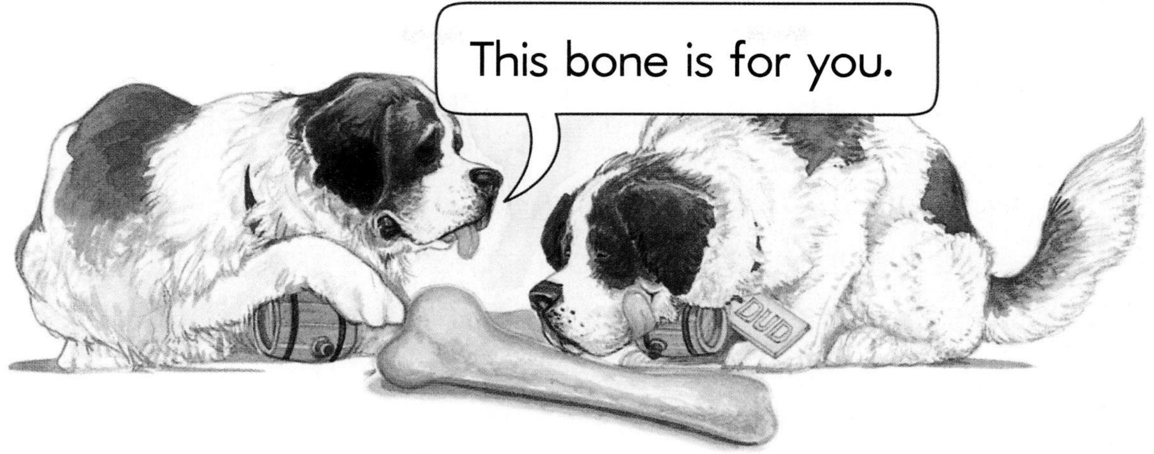

The dogs were very tired. They just ate a little bit and curled up in their beds. Dud was starting to fall asleep when the oldest dog said, "I want to thank Dud for doing what he did. He saved a mountain climber. And he did more than that."

All the other dogs looked up and waited for the oldest dog to say more. "He showed what he can do when he really puts his mind to it. He showed us that he's going to be pretty good at his job."

The other dogs said, "Yeah, pretty good."

Just then, the ranger came back and thanked the dogs. He left some meat scraps and a large ham bone. After the ranger left, the oldest dog picked up the ham bone and took it over to Dud. He said, "This is for you."

Dud started to say, "Well, I really don't think I should . . ." He was going to tell them that he shouldn't have the bone, but it smelled so good that he stopped talking and started to do something else. Yum, yum, yum.

The end.

Sharks are hunters of the sea. Sharks are fish, and they are very strong. But they are different from most fish. Most fish have teeth that are like your teeth and bones that are like your bones. Sharks do not have teeth like yours. The teeth of a shark are really just scales. The bones of sharks are not like your bones.

Real bone holds up the part of your nose near your face. Grab your nose near your face, just below your eyes. Move it from side to side. Does real bone bend?

The same stuff sharks' bones are made of holds up the tip of your nose. Grab the tip of your nose and move it from side to side. Do sharks' bones bend?

1. Are sharks fish?
2. The teeth of the shark are really ______.
3. A shark's bones are made of the same stuff that holds up the tip of your ______.
4. Does real bone bend?
5. Do sharks' bones bend?

oo
a
i
o
1. willing
2. snoring
3. boring
4. either
5. except
6. polite
1. patient
2. certain
3. clinic
4. practice
5. trouble
1. Bill Wilson
2. Milly
3. minute
4. expert
5. asleep
6. bell
1. popular
2. school
3. sure
4. wife
5. answer
6. parents

Boring Bill
Part One

Bill Wilson was a nice man. He was kind to dogs, cats, and other animals. He took good care of his car, his house, and his lawn. He loved his wife, Milly, and he liked people. He was always willing to help people when they needed help, and he was very polite.

Bill Wilson did all of these nice things, but he still was not a very popular person. You see, Bill was boring. He was so boring that every time he started talking, he would put people to sleep. Within a few minutes, people would either be yawning or leaving the room. Within a few more minutes, anybody who stayed in the room would be snoring.

Bill once gave a talk to parents at a school. After only ten minutes, everybody except Bill was asleep. The room was very noisy because people were snoring so loudly. After the meeting, one woman said, "We were snoring because Bill is boring." From that day on, people called Bill Wilson "Boring Bill." They didn't say it to his face, but they said it. And Bill knew about it.

One evening, Bill said to his wife, "The more I speak, the more people sleep. There must be something I can do to be less boring, but I'm not sure what it is. Tell me, Milly, what should I do to be less boring?"

Milly didn't answer him, because she was sound asleep. Bill looked at her and said to himself, "I must do something to change the way I talk. I am tired of being so boring."

More to come.

Jen liked to make things, but the things she made didn't fit. Once she made a hat for her brother. That hat went over his ears, his eyes, his nose, his mouth, and his neck. He said, "This hat is so big, it could be a bag."

He cut three holes in it. One hole was on top. The other two holes were on the sides. He gave the hat to a little girl and said, "Here is a fine dress for you."

She loved that dress.

1. Who liked to make things?
2. Did the things she made fit well?
3. What did she make for her brother?
4. Was that hat too big or too small?
5. How many holes did he cut in the hat?
6. Now that hat is a ______.

31

1. baby
2. story
3. lady
4. babies
5. stories
6. ladies
1. amazing
2. listening
3. speaking
4. young
5. piece
1. move
2. rang
3. bounce
4. blub
1. finished
2. explaining
3. difference
4. changes
5. certainly
6. practicing
1. interest
2. normal
3. mirror
4. wasting

Boring Bill
Part Two

Bill tried to say things that would interest other people. He asked questions and tried to get people to talk about themselves. He tried to say things that were funny. He tried to talk faster and louder. He tried to smile more when he talked. But all those changes made no difference. After Bill was through speaking, everybody else was sleeping.

One day, Bill was at home. He was practicing in front of the mirror. He smiled, moved around a lot, and talked to the mirror.

Just then the door bell rang. Bill opened the door and saw a woman who said, “I am an expert at making people sleep. I work for the Sleep More Clinic. We help people who have trouble sleeping. I hear that you can make people sleep, too.”

“Yes,” Bill said. “If I speak for a while, people will sleep.”

“That is interesting,” the sleep expert said. “Can you explain how you make people sleep?”

“Yes, I can,” Bill said. “It seems that I am boring.” Bill went on to explain why he was boring and tell about some things that happened to him. When Bill finished explaining his problem, he noticed that the sleep expert was snoring.

Bill woke the expert up. The expert said, "Oh, dear. I don't know what came over me. I was listening to what you said, and then . . . "

Bill said, "Oh, I understand. That happens to me all the time."

The expert said, "Do you mind if I come back tomorrow with some other experts from the clinic?"

"No, I don't mind."

After the expert left, Bill made up his mind that he would be interesting when the others visited him. He said to himself, "They will not be able to fall asleep."

More to come.

I have four legs, two arms, and a back. I stand about four feet high, and I am made mostly of wood. My legs are stiff, and they hold me up.

I have a padded seat where people can sit. People rest their arms on my arms. I will stay where you put me, but I don't like to be left alone for a long time. Please sit on me.

1. What kind of thing is telling this story?
   - a car
   - a chair
   - a dog
2. Name the part that is padded.
3. What do people do with this thing?
4. What does this thing want you to do?

?

?

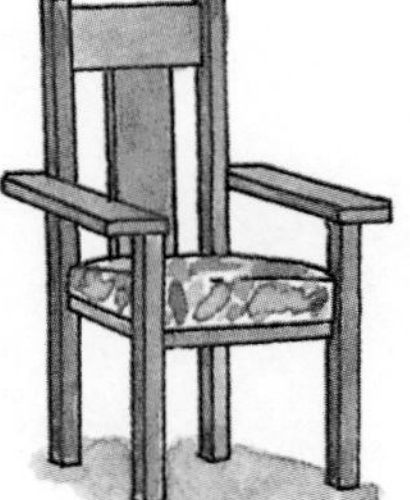

?

32

1. stories
2. babies
3. ponies
4. parties
1. honking
2. wasting
3. amazing
4. certain
5. certainly
1. young
2. guy
3. thirty
4. twenty
5. normal
6. patients
1. bottle
2. bother
3. finger
4. finish
5. message
6. write

Boring Bill
Part Three

Nine experts from the Sleep More Clinic were on their way to visit Bill. One of them kept arguing with the others. She said, "I don't believe those stories about how Bill is able to make people sleep. We know more about putting people to sleep than he knows. After all, we are experts. Bill is not an expert, so Bill can't know more about sleep than we know. I think we are wasting our time."

The woman who visited Bill the day before said, "We are not wasting our time."

The leader of the team said, "Now, now. Let's not argue. We'll listen to what Bill has to say. I want everybody to take notes and ask good questions."

When they got to Bill's place, they asked Bill to explain how he put people to sleep. He said, "When I talk in my normal voice, people just fall asleep. But today, I'm talking in a voice that will keep all of you wide awake. I have been working on this voice, and it is very interesting. It is not like my normal voice, which is soft and easy. This voice has a lot of bounce. I think you'll see that . . . "

One of the experts said, "Zzzz."

Another expert said, "Snort, blub, zzzz."

The woman who believed that she knew more about putting people to sleep than Bill did said, "Gl gl honk zzzzzzz."

Bill stopped talking and waited for the others to wake up. The first one to wake up was the leader. "Oh my," he said as he looked at the others. "That was amazing. You certainly do know how to put people to sleep."

After a while, all the experts except one were awake. The only one who kept on honking and snoring was the expert who thought she knew more about putting people to sleep than Bill did.

She woke up when the experts were getting ready to leave. She said, "Well, let's begin the meeting."

The leader said, "We're through meeting."

More next time.

There once was a big piece of ice that didn't like the cold. That ice was in an ice box. One day the ice said, "I'm tired of being cold. I will go where it is warm."

The other pieces of ice in the ice box said, "But if you go where it is warm, you will melt."

But the piece didn't listen to the others. That piece of ice left the ice box. Soon the piece noticed that it was getting smaller. The piece of ice said, "I must go back to the ice box."

And it did. Now the piece does not hate the cold. That piece says, "I am smaller but wiser."

1. What didn't the piece of ice like?
2. Where did the ice live?
3. Who tried to warn the piece of ice about leaving the ice box?
4. They told the big piece that it would ______.
5. Did the piece of ice leave the ice box?
6. Did the piece of ice return to the ice box?
7. Is the piece of ice bigger or smaller?

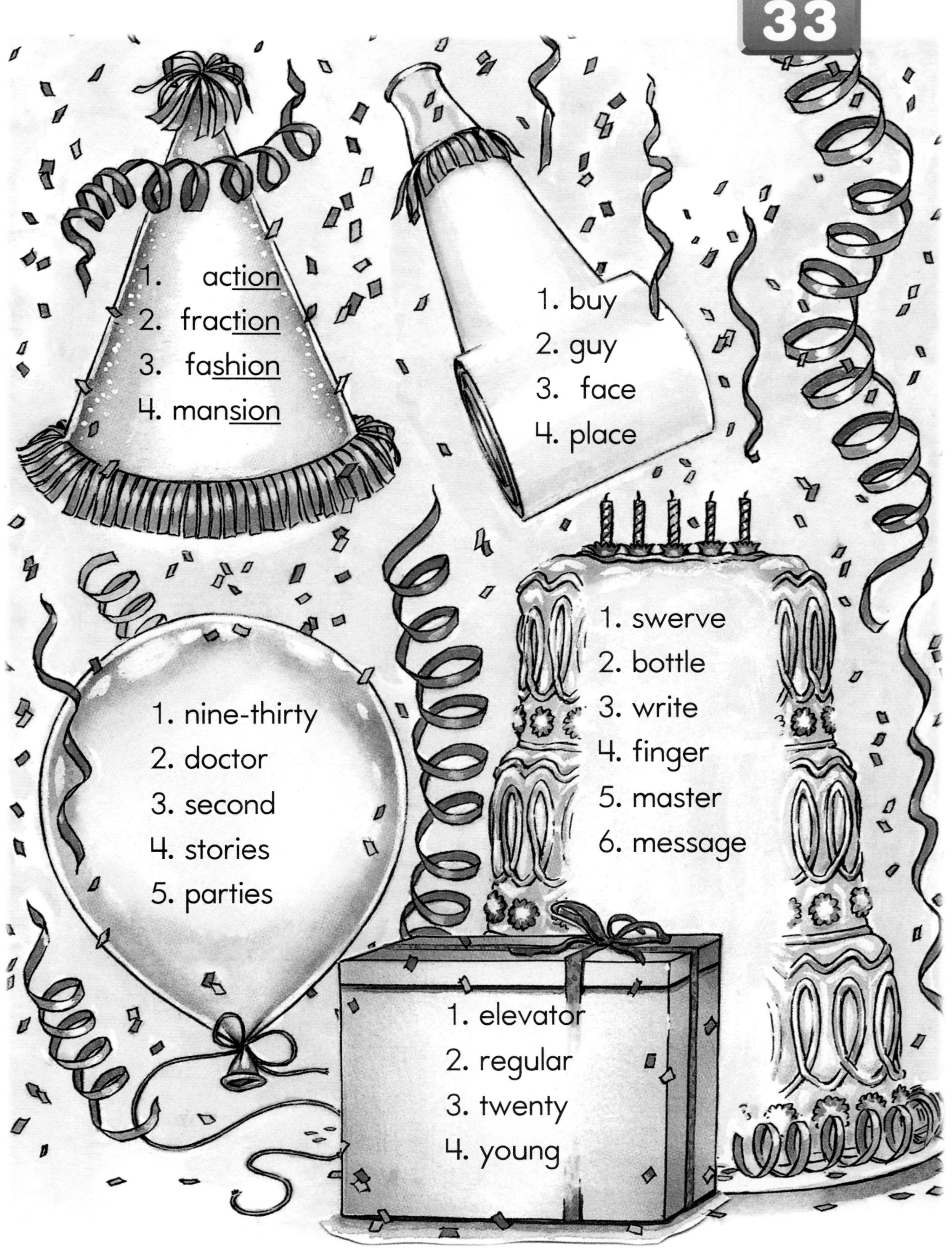
1. action
2. fraction
3. fashion
4. mansion
1. buy
2. guy
3. face
4. place
1. nine-thirty
2. doctor
3. second
4. stories
5. parties
1. swerve
2. bottle
3. write
4. finger
5. master
6. message
1. elevator
2. regular
3. twenty
4. young

Boring Bill
Part Four

When the nine experts from the Sleep More Clinic left Bill's place, he felt very sad. He had tried to be interesting, but his plan had not worked.

Later that day, Bill felt a lot better. He got a call from the leader of the team. The leader said, "Bill, could you come to the Sleep More Clinic tomorrow? You may be able to help us with some people who have not been able to sleep."

So the next morning at nine-thirty, Bill was at the clinic. The leader told Bill that the first patient he would see had not been able to sleep for three nights. When that patient came in, she said, "Nobody can help me sleep. What's the point of talking to another doctor? I know I won't sleep tonight either."

Bill said, "I'm not a doctor. I'm just a boring kind of guy."

The patient said, "So now I don't even get to talk to a doctor."

Bill said, "Well, you don't really have to talk. All you have to do is listen to what I say. I'll talk for a while, and before you know . . . "

"Snort. Zzzz."

The same thing happened with the next patient, a young woman who had not been able to sleep for nearly a week.

After Bill put the second patient to sleep, the leader said, "Why are we working with patients one at a time? Let's bring in all the other patients and see what happens."

So twenty patients came in. Bill talked to them for five minutes, and the room was filled with the sounds of people snorting, snoring, honking, and making lots of **Z**s. The sounds came from twenty patients with sleep problems and four doctors from the Sleep More Clinic who had been watching Bill work.

Before Bill left, the leader of the sleep team asked Bill, "Would you like to work at our clinic?"

We'll find out more next time.

Steve wanted to climb a mountain. He didn't know which trail to take, but he was afraid to ask anyone. He didn't want people to think he wasn't smart. So he didn't ask any questions.

Steve picked a trail and started up it. Soon the trail became steep and rocky. Before Steve knew it, he was standing on the edge of a cliff. Steve was stuck. So a ranger had to come with ropes to pull Steve off the cliff. The ranger said, "Why did you take that trail?" Steve didn't know what to say.

Later Steve told himself, "Next time, I'll ask questions."

1. What did Steve want to climb?
2. Did Steve know which trail to take?
3. Did he ask anybody which trail to take?
4. Steve got stuck on a ______.
5. Will Steve ask questions next time?

tion aw ou sion shion ew
1. mention
2. action
3. vision
4. nation
1. island
2. added
3. size
4. inch
5. grown
6. maker
1. strange
2. regular
3. swerve
4. elevator
1. driver
2. faces
3. spiders
4. added
5. hardly
6. throwing
1. bear
2. giant
3. ago
4. using
5. father
6. full

Boring Bill
Part Five

Bill had a new job at the Sleep More Clinic, and Bill was the star sleep maker. He would work with people who couldn't sleep. After he talked to them for a few minutes, they were making **Z**s with big smiles on their faces.

Bill was the star, but he still had problems. One day, he started talking to people in the elevator. When he got off the elevator, everybody else was asleep. One time after work, he started talking to the bus driver as the bus moved along the street. Soon the bus started to swerve. The driver was asleep. Bill woke the driver up just in time.

Bill kept reading books about how to be interesting, and Bill kept trying different things. At last, he found something that worked. He talked in a high voice and talked faster. Nobody fell asleep. He could talk to the people in the elevator, and they wouldn't fall asleep. He could talk to bus drivers without putting them to sleep.

But Bill's high voice did not work with his patients. When he talked to them in his high voice, they just looked at him and said, "This is not working. I am still awake."

So now Bill has two voices. He talks in his regular voice when he is working with patients. But when he is not at work, he speaks in a high voice. That voice sounds a little strange, but it doesn't put his wife or his friends to sleep. In fact, Bill is pretty popular, and people no longer call him Boring Bill. They call him the Sleep Master.

The end.

Before the moose and the goose met, the moose was bothered because he had a bug on his back. That bug kept biting him. He tried many ways to get rid of the bug. He rolled in the dirt. He rubbed his back against trees. He dove under water. But none of the things the moose did stopped that bug from biting him.

At last the moose yelled, "I hate bugs."

The goose was walking by and heard the moose. The goose said, "I don't hate bugs. I love them."

That goose hopped up on the moose's back and ate the bug. That made the moose happy, and that made the goose happy. After that, the moose and the goose became good friends.

1. What kept biting the moose?
2. Who hated bugs?
3. Who loved bugs?
4. What did the goose do with the bug?
5. How did that make the moose feel?

35

Bottles are made from glass. Glass is strange. When glass is very hot, it starts to get red and very soft. As it gets hotter, it starts to melt, just like a candy bar melts on a hot day.

Bottles are made from hot melted glass. The glass goes into a mold that is the shape of the bottle. Then air is blown inside to push the glass against the sides of the mold. When the hot glass cools, there is a bottle inside the mold.

1. What are bottles made from?
2. What happens to glass when it gets very hot?
3. To make a bottle, hot glass goes into a ______.
4. When the glass cools, what is left inside the mold?

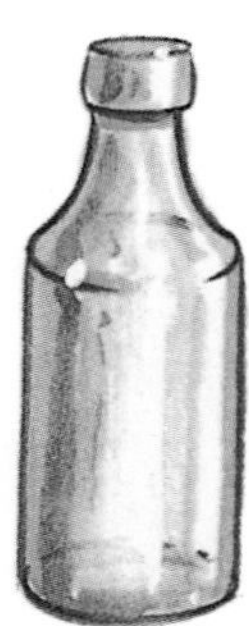